Distributed by Columbia House, 51 West 52nd Street, New York, New York 10019
Printed in U.S.A.

## ACKNOWLEDGMENTS

Permission to reprint has been kindly granted by Alfred A. Knopf, Inc. *(A History of National Socialism, Hitler: A Biography)*; Allan Wingate (Publishers) Ltd *(Young Hitler: The Story of Our Friendship)*; Burke Publishing Company Ltd. *(Hitler Was My Friend)*; Coward, McCann & Geoghegan, Inc. *(Hitler: The Last Ten Days)*; David Higham Associates, Ltd. *(The Revolution of Nihilism: Warning to the West)*; Doubleday & Company, Inc. *(The Goebbels Diaries: 1942-1943)*; Farrar, Straus & Giroux, Inc. *(Hitler's Secret Conversations, 1941-1944)*; Harcourt Brace Jovanovich, Inc. *(Hitler)*; Harper & Row, Publishers, Inc. *(Hitler: A Study in Tyranny)*; Hoover Institution Press *(Adolf Hitler: His Family, Childhood and Youth)*; Houghton Mifflin Company *(Hitler and I, Mein Kampf, Der Fuehrer: Hitler's Rise to Power)*; Hutchinson Publishing Group Ltd. *(Hitler's Youth)*; The John Day Company, Inc. *(Secret Conversations with Hitler: The Two Newly-Discovered 1931 Interviews)*; Le Figaro; Macmillan Publishing Co., Inc. *(The Last Days of Hitler, Inside the Third Reich)*; The New Republic, Inc. ("The Hitler Boom" by Charles Lam); Newsweek, Inc.; The New Yorker Magazine, Inc. (Notes and Comment in *The New Yorker* of December 20, 1941); The New York Times Company; Oxford University Press *(The Speeches of Adolf Hitler)*; Praeger Publishers, Inc. *(The German Dictatorship: The Origins, Structure, and Effects of National Socialism)*; Public Affairs Press *(Hitler's Words)*; Simon & Schuster, Inc. *(The Rise and Fall of the Third Reich)*; St. Louis Post-Dispatch; St. Martin's Press, Inc., Macmillan & Co., Ltd. *(The Nemesis of Power)*; Time Inc. *(Time, The Weekly Newsmagazine)*; Oceana Publications, Inc. *(Sieg Heil! The Story of Adolf Hitler)*; Princeton University Press *(Hitler and the Beer Hall Putsch)*; Oswald Wolff (Publishers) Ltd. *(Adolf Hitler)*; Harper & Row, Publishers, Inc. *(Hitler: Legend, Myth and Reality)*.

## PICTURE CREDITS

Cover: Wide World; p. 4: Brown Bros.; p. 7: Bettman; p. 15: Photoworld; p. 22: Brown Bros.; p. 31: Wide World; p. 38: Photoworld; p. 44: Photoworld; p. 51: Photoreporters; p. 62: Culver; p. 64: Bettman; p. 68: Photoworld; p. 70: Photoworld; p. 73: Photoworld, Photoreporters; p. 77: Wide World, Photoworld; p. 82: Photoreporters, Photoworld; p. 84: Wide World, Photoworld; p. 88: UPI; p. 91: Wide World; p. 95: Pictorial Parade; p. 99: Wide World; p. 100: Photoworld; p. 101; Culver; p. 105: Photoreporters; p. 107: Photoreporters; p. 108: Culver; p. 110: Sovfoto; p. 111: Keystone Press; p. 113: Granger Collection; p. 114: Pictorial Parade; p. 119: Photoworld; p. 122: Culver; p. 123: Culver; p. 126: Brown Bros.; p. 127: Pictorial Parade; p. 130: Brown Bros.; p. 131: Wide World, Photoreporters; p. 133: Brown Bros.; p. 136: Photoworld; p. 140: Keystone Press; p. 144: Sovfoto, Pictorial Parade; p. 148: Wide World; p. 150: Brown Bros.; p. 154: Culver; p. 162: Keystone Press, p. 165: Photoworld; p. 171: Photoworld; p. 172: Magnum.

# CONTENTS

# 1
# THE YOUNG HITLER

Adolf Hitler, who was to become the most feared and hated human being since Attila the Hun, was born on April 20, 1889, to middle-class parents in Braunau am Inn, Austria, a village on the frontier that separates Austria and the German state of Bavaria.

His father, Alois, then 50, was a customs official, a minor but respectable status. Severe in appearance, burly, and totally bald, Alois Hitler was an inflexible, arrogant tyrant. Adolf's mother was of an entirely different nature. Klara Pölzl, 28 years old when Adolf was born, was a gentle, humble woman, long-limbed and pretty, with large, luminous eyes.

Neither Klara nor Alois was a native of Braunau. They had come there from the Waldviertel, the wooded, billowing region lying between the Danube and the Bohemian-Moravian border.

Waldviertel was heavily inbred. Marriages among first and second cousins were common. Klara's great-grandfather was Alois's grandfather. Thus, Alois and Klara were distant cousins and, in accordance with their Roman Catholic faith, had to obtain papal dispensation for their marriage.

What attracted Klara to this difficult, older man is difficult to determine. His background was hardly auspicious. Alois was born out of wedlock and his father, Johann Georg Hiedler, did not recognize him as his lawful son. Hiedler married Alois's mother, Maria Anna Schicklgruber, after Alois was born, then promptly abandoned both of them to resume his existence as an itinerant miller and inveterate drunkard. His mother cared for Alois while working as a servant. She died when Alois was 10, and he was raised by an uncle.

Alois Schicklgruber became a cobbler and, at 39, married a well-to-do woman 14 years his senior, who purchased a position for him in the Austrian civil service. This allowed him to wear a uniform, in which he proudly posed for photographs in a military stance. She even purchased the legal papers that

## A REFLECTION OF THE TIMES

• In Hitler there is a great deal of what Walter Benjamin called "social character." That is, he incorporated all the anxieties, protests, and hopes of the age in his own self to a remarkable degree. But in him all emotions were enormously exaggerated, distorted, and infiltrated with weird features, though never unrelated or incongruent to the historical background. Consequently, Hitler's life would hardly deserve the telling if it were not that extrapersonal tendencies or conditions came to light in it; his biography is essentially part of the biography of the age. And because his life was inextricably linked to his time, it is worth the telling.

*Joachim C. Fest, 1973* [6a]

## BORN IN A SMALL
## BORDER COMMUNITY

• Braunau was then a little border com-

munity of approximately 3,500 people. The town was seventy-eight miles southeast of Munich, on a secondary route to Vienna. By train the trip from Braunau to the Bavarian capital took between four and five hours. Some trade and a few tourists passed through the town, but it was primarily a center for the agricultural districts between Passau and Salzburg. The buildings of Braunau were constructed along the banks of the river Inn and gave the impression of being strung out along the bed of the stream. The dull line of medium-sized buildings was broken only by the Stephanskirche, with its large baroque cupola. . . .

The location of Adolf Hitler's birthplace on the river Inn bordering Austria and Germany provided a basis for unlimited propaganda in later years. Hitler himself worked hard to wring every ounce of political advantage from the accident of his birthplace. However, the town's influence on the "drummer from Braunau on the Inn" could not have been extensive.

*Bradley F. Smith, 1967* [32a]

allowed him to use his father's name, which he smoothed out from Hiedler to Hitler. From poverty and an orphan's existence, Alois had become a respected, moneyed citizen.

Alois's wife died after six years of marriage. In six weeks time he remarried, this time a pretty cook who already had born him an illegitimate son. She was tubercular, however, and died a year later. Again, Alois, a man who needed the company of a woman, did not mourn long. He married Klara Pölzl three short months after his second wife's death.

Alois had known Klara as a child. Her first job, at the age of 10, was as a maid in the home of his wealthy first wife. Klara

## HITLER'S PARENTS

• In this little town on the Inn, gilded by the rays of German martyrdom, Bavarian by blood, technically Austrian, lived my parents in the late eighties of the past century; my father a dutiful civil servant, my mother giving all her being to the household, and devoted above all to us children in eternal, loving care. Little remains in my memory of this period, for after a few years my father had to leave the little border city he had learned to love, moving down the Inn to take a new position in Passau, that is, in Germany proper.

*Adolf Hitler, 1924* [11a]

• As a homeless young man, Alois Hitler learned the shoemaker's trade; but his ardent desire was to become an official. The legend of the rise of the small man! Alois Hitler has been described as a stern, correct, industrious, punctual, and clearheaded man; in many things, the exact opposite of his son. In his struggle to attain the dignity of an official is expressed the yearning and the fear of life of that huge section of the population which was later to support National Socialism. Alois Hitler, with his longing for rank and an assured livelihood, was already a part of the Hitler movement. Not until he was forty years of age and after long wandering through the Austrian world did he achieve his end. He became a customs official.

*Konrad Heiden, 1936* [10a]

• Intelligence, in a woman, is not an essential thing. My mother, for example, would have cut a poor figure in the society of our cultivated women. She lived strictly for her husband and children. They were her entire universe. But she gave a son to Germany.

*Hitler, March 11, 1942* [12a]

• . . . this woman who was to bring

Young Adolf

bore Alois four sons and two daughters. Adolf, who was to enslave most of Europe and be responsible for the death of millions of people on battlefields and in ovens, was the only son to survive into manhood.

The family lived in Braunau am Inn until 1892, when they moved to Passau. They lived in this Bavarian community until 1895, when Alois bought a farm near Lambach. For two years, Adolf attended the Benedictine monastery at Lambach, where he distinguished himself in the choir. Alois decided that he could live on his pension and savings, without having to work. The Hitlers moved to Leonding, near Linz.

Adolf Hitler into the world emerges as the most compelling and sympathetic figure in the annals of the family. She lived her life under inauspicious circumstances and saw her hopes and dreams steadily come to naught over a span of twenty years. Yet in spite of all the blows she had to bear, she quietly returned again and again to fulfill her obligations humanely and conscientiously. She was a fairly large girl, almost as tall as her husband, with dark brown hair and even features. Her life was centered on the tasks of maintaining her home and caring for her husband and the children of the family. . . . Everyone who knew her agreed that it was in her love and devotion for the children that Klara's life centered. The only serious charge ever raised against her is that because of this love and devotion she was over-indulgent and thus encouraged a sense of uniqueness in her son—a somewhat strange charge to be brought against a mother. The children did not share this view. Her stepchildren and her own offspring who survived infancy loved and respected their mother.

*Bradley F. Smith, 1967* [32b]

## THE FAMILY MOVES

• In August 1892, when Adolf was three years and four months old, his family moved to Passau in Lower Bavaria, where they remained until April 1895. . . .

. . . Thus in the most impressionable period of his childhood Adolf was among German, not Austrian, children, not only copying their speech, but feeling himself one of them.

*Franz Jetzinger, 1958* [15a]

## ALOIS BECOMES MORE CROTCHETY AND IRRITABLE

• His moods increased family tensions and made life more burdensome for everyone. The oldest child, fourteen-year-old

The Hitler household was not a happy one, and the blame appears to lie with the testy disposition of the formidable Alois. Now in his fifties and, with his drinking and other bad habits, he was both unfit and in no mood to look after a young boy. Prone to violence, he would thrash his son unmercifully for almost any reason.

Alois strove to groom Adolf for the Austrian civil service. Adolf was to follow in his father's steps and become a customs officer wearing a velvet cap with a gold service stripe. But the boy—a dreamer, avid reader, and given to roaming the fields alone—decided he wanted to be an artist.

Alois, was the first to succumb. In 1896 he left home. His departure caused a violent controversy with his father. . . .

. . . After his departure, Adolf became the chief target of his father's anger. All the old man's toil and sacrifice had been wasted on the older son. Adolf, now the oldest boy in the household, had to assume added responsibility at a time when he already was hard pressed to meet the demands of home and school. Alois' ambition led him to promote the competitive virtues in his children, but at the same time he required absolute subordination to his authority. This demand for a combination of self-reliance and obedience was a common source of conflict in the middle class of a half a century ago. The conflict was pronounced in Alois' case because of his early retirement and the immaturity of many of his children. He was especially vulnerable to pressure created by conflicts in his value system, and his resulting restlessness and moodiness compounded the difficulties of his seven-year-old son.

*Bradley F. Smith, 1967* [32c]

## A BOY AT PLAY

• He was out of doors almost continually [in Leonding], playing with a gang of boys. With his town upbringing, Adolf was quicker-witted than they and was the instigator of all their pranks. They often played the popular children's game, 'Cops and Robbers,' and the fringe of the nearby Kürnberger forest was ideal ground, offering plenty of hide-outs. . . .

Adolf, I was told, was never a fighter. He used his tongue instead of his fists. He was more alert than the other boys and in their games it was he who used his wits to best advantage. War games were always Adolf's favourite and he was always the leader in them.

*Franz Jetzinger, 1958* [15b]

Adolf Hitler in elementary school. He stands in the center of the top row (and is indicated by an "x" above his head).

Adolf had been a fairly diligent and obedient pupil through grammar school. His first year of high school was discouraging. He failed and had to repeat the grade. His father reprimanded him harshly for not paying attention to his schooling. Adolf retorted that he wanted to be an artist, but, under no circumstances, a customs official. The father-son confrontations threw the household in constant upheaval. Klara tried her best to ease the situation.

Adolf often escaped into his reading. About this time, he came across a German history book extolling the glories of the Franco-Prussian War. He also encountered a history teacher

who argued persuasively for the spread of German influence throughout Europe. At age 12, Adolf became a Pan-Germanist. He had "learned to understand and penetrate into the true sense of history," he later said.

In January, 1903, old Alois Hitler collapsed and died while sipping wine at a local tavern. After his burial, his wife sold the house in Leonding and moved to Linz. Her pension was sufficient to support her teenage son and his younger sister.

Adolf's dependence on his mother deepened. In analyzing Hitler's psychological makeup in the 1930s, John Gunther concluded that the dictator had a mother complex. He "is still an

## SCHOOL DAYS

• In my day, pupils were not only compelled to achieve a given average, but also in certain branches their reports must not fall below a minimum level. If a pupil is particularly brilliant in his specialty, why embarrass him in his studies by obliging him to assimilate notions that are beyond his powers of assimilation? Wouldn't it be better to help him further in the direction that comes naturally to him?

Forty years ago, the teaching of history was restricted to a dry listing of dates. There was a total absence of principles. What happened when the teacher, into the bargain, lacked the necessary gift for giving these dead things a soul? Such teaching was a real torture....

When I think of the men who were my teachers, I realize that most of them were slightly mad. The men who could be regarded as good teachers were exceptional. It's tragic to think that such people have the power to bar a young man's way. . . .

I remember that on the average I spent a tenth of the time my comrades spent in doing my prep. My selected branch was history. I felt sorry for those of my comrades who never had a minute for play. Some children begin their school careers as excellent book-learners. They pass the barrage of examinations brilliantly. In their own eyes, everything is at their feet. So what a surprise it is for them when they see a comrade succeeding who is cleverer than they are, but whom they used to regard as a dunce!

*Hitler, March 3, 1942* [12y]

• With few exceptions he disliked his teachers, finding them unsympathetic and dull. He was particularly unhappy about their appearance, which he later described as sloppy, "with dirty collars, unkempt beards and the like." This opinion, reflecting some middle-class fastidiousness, combined with his low performance to lessen teacher interest in him. To the teachers, Adolf appeared a "cantankerous"

emotional slave to the dreams of his childhood, still chained by an immense bond to the woman who was the most important factor in his personal life—his mother."

In the spring of 1905, Adolf made his first trip to Vienna—a two-week sojourn during which he fell in love with the dazzling city. In the fall of 1907, he again went to Vienna. Then, in December, 1907, Adolf's mother, who had been sickly for years, died of cancer. Hitler was on his own.

His mother's death was a traumatic experience for young Hitler. August Kubizek, one of his few close friends, wrote in his book, *The Young Hitler*, that "Adolf really loved his mother. . . .

and "lazy" lad who did not cooperate and resented reproof.

*Bradley F. Smith, 1967* [32d]

• What made our good fortune all the greater was that this teacher [Dr. Leopold Pötsch, Hitler's professor at the *Realschule*] knew how to illuminate the past by examples from the present, and how from the past to draw inferences for the present. As a result he had more understanding than anyone else for all the daily problems which then held us breathless. He used our budding nationalistic fanaticism as a means of educating us, frequently appealing to our sense of national honor. By this alone he was able to discipline us little ruffians more easily than would have been possible by any other means.

This teacher made history my favorite subject.

And indeed, though he had no such intention, it was then that I became a little revolutionary.

For who could have studied German history under such a teacher without becoming an enemy of the state which, through its ruling house, exerted so disastrous an influence on the destinies of the nation?

And who could retain his loyalty to a dynasty which in past and present betrayed the needs of the German people again and again for shameless private advantage?

*Hitler, 1924* [11b]

• Already in Linz, Adolf had started to read the classics. Of Goethe's "Faust" he once remarked that it contained more than the human mind could grasp. Once we saw . . . the rarely performed second part. . . . Adolf was very moved and spoke of it for a long time. It is natural that, of Schiller's works, "Wilhelm Tell" affected him most deeply. On the other hand, strange to relate, he did not like "Die Räuber" very much. He was profoundly impressed by Dante's Divine Comedy although, to my mind, he was much too young when he read it.

*August Kubizek, 1954* [16b]

I remember many occasions when he showed this love for his mother, most deeply and movingly during her last illness; he never spoke of his mother but with deep affection. He was a good son." [16a]

Hitler always had tended to be idle and romantic. Now he spent more time rhapsodizing about art, history, and love. In 1907, before his mother died, he had applied unsuccessfully for acceptance to the Vienna Academy of Fine Arts. He had convinced himself that his flair for drawing was a genuine talent. He remembered bitterly, as he wrote in *Mein Kampf*, that when he informed his father of his ambitions, Alois cried, "Artist!

### AGAINST HIS FATHER'S WISHES

• Then barely eleven years old, I was forced into opposition for the first time in my life. Hard and determined as my father might be in putting through plans and purposes once conceived, his son was just as persistent and recalcitrant in rejecting an idea which appealed to him not at all, or in any case very little.

I did not want to become a civil servant.

Neither permission nor 'serious' arguments made any impression on my resistance. I did not want to be a civil servant, no, and again no. All attempts on my father's part to inspire me with love or pleasure in this profession by stories from his own life accomplished the exact opposite. I yawned and grew sick to my stomach at the thought of sitting in an office, deprived of my liberty; ceasing to be master of my own time and being compelled to force the content of a whole life into blanks that had to be filled out. . . .

. . . I wanted to become a painter and no power in the world could make me a civil servant. . . .

. . . my mother finally consented to take me out of the *Realschule* and let me attend the Academy.

These were the happiest days of my life and seemed to me almost a dream; and a mere dream it was to remain. Two years later, the death of my mother put a sudden end to all my high-flown plans.

It was the conclusion of a long and painful illness which from the beginning left little hope of recovery. Yet it was a dreadful blow, particularly for me. I had honored my father, but my mother I had loved.

*Hitler, 1924* [11c]

• Adolf spoke of his father with great respect. I never heard him say anything against him, in spite of their differences of opinion about his career. Adolf did not take it amiss that his father had autocratically decided on his son's future career; for this he considered his right, even his duty.

*August Kubizek, 1954* [16c]

Not as long as I live. Never!"

In 1908, Adolf took the academy entrance examination once more. Again rejected, he complained to friends about "injustice" and forced an interview with the academy's vice-chancellor. It did no good. He tried the School of Architecture and met another setback. These rejections were blows to his confidence. They struck at the one seeming ability in which he took huge pride. For years, he was to remember this insult by the "establishment."

With his mother gone, there was nothing to hold Hitler in Linz. "Determined to become 'something,' but certainly not a

### A MIDDLE-CLASS FAMILY

• Economically the Hitlers belonged to the elevated middle class. Neither before nor in the five years following the father's death was there any question of "need"— all stories to this effect had an ulterior motive. When Hitler's mother sold her house in Leonding in the summer of 1905 and moved into the town itself she received as the net price nearly 7,500 kronen and this was in addition to her widow's pension which, as her husband had reached the highest rank possible to him in the Custom Service, was quite substantial.

*Helmut Heiber, 1960* [13a]

### ADOLF'S FATHER DIES

• The great force which had determined the conditions under which he lived was gone. He immediately gained more freedom and saw his position within the family enhanced. Klara did not allow Alois' ideals and goals to perish completely. She used his memory as her strongest support in guiding the boy, but her pleading and urging was a pale shadow of the old patriarch's mandates. All Klara really wanted, in contrast to the set program of her husband, was for the boy to finish school, make something of himself, and be happy.

*Bradley F. Smith, 1967* [32e]

### A HOME FOR SCHOOLBOYS

• In the semester that followed Alois' death . . . a new arrangement was made for Adolf's schooling in order to get him through a difficult adjustment period without further damage to his academic record. Klara placed him in a home for schoolboys (*Kostplatz*) in Linz, where he lived during the week and then came home to Leonding on the weekend. Adolf was polite but reserved to the woman who ran the home . . . and also to the five children who stayed there. He never broke through the formal form of address (*Sie*) with any of them, and spent most of his time reading and drawing. In school his record, as usual,

civil servant," he wrote, he headed for Vienna.

At the turn of the century, Vienna was a metropolis with a population of two million. As the capital of the Austro-Hungarian Empire, the city was living out the final years of its carefree, gay existence. It was a city of waltzes and operettas, cafés and concerts, duels and sophisticated scandals. The "beautiful Blue Danube" seemed symbolic of the serenity and confidence of a rich, powerful empire.

But these aspects of Vienna could only be glimpsed by young Hitler, who was, like the proverbial country boy, making his way in the big city. His place was with the million or more

was barely passing, and he failed mathematics, which meant that he had to take another makeup examination in the fall in order to advance to the third class.

*Bradley F. Smith, 1967* [32f]

### DEATH OF A BELOVED MOTHER

● On the 23rd of December, 1907, I went with my mother to the house of mourning. . . . a glance at [Adolf's] face was sufficient to know how he had suffered in those hours. Not only had he now lost both his parents, but with his mother he had lost the only creature on earth on whom he had concentrated his love, and who had loved him in return. . . .

. . . He had a horror of going alone, because this, his third journey to Vienna, was a quite different proposition from his earlier visits. Then, he still had his mother, and though he was away, his home still existed. He was not then taking a step into the unknown, for the knowl-

edge that his mother was waiting to welcome him with open arms at any time and in any circumstances gave a firm and reliable substance to his insecure life. His home was the quiet centre round which his stormy existence revolved. Now he had lost it. Going to Vienna would be the last and final decision from which there was no turning back—a jump into the dark.

*August Kubizek, 1954* [16d]

### VIENNA IN THE EARLY 1900's

● . . . for all its contemporaneity and show, Vienna was already a "world of yesterday"—full of scruples, decrepitude, and deep-seated doubts about itself. As the twentieth century began, the brilliance displayed in its theaters, its bourgeois mansions and green boulevards was overhung by this eschatological mood. Amid all the lavish festivals the city celebrated in fact and fiction there was palpable awareness that the age had lost its vital

laborers and workers who could barely subsist, and the horde of outcasts, vagabonds, and criminals who filled the capital's alleys and streets. From 1908 until just before the outbreak of World War I in 1914, this was to be his home. For Hitler, they were years of humiliation and poverty, years he later called the saddest of his life. "Even today," he wrote in *Mein Kampf*, "the city calls forth none but gloomy thoughts for me."

Hitler did whatever he could to earn a krone here and there: sweeping snow in the winter, carrying luggage for people at the railway depot, painting small pictures, doing odd manual jobs. He slept in the big dormitory of a public shelter in the

force, that only a lovely semblance still survived. Weariness, defeats anxieties, the more and more embittered quarrels among the nations of the empire, and the short-sightedness of the ruling groups were eroding the unwieldy structure. Nowhere else in old Europe was the atmosphere of termination and exhaustion so palpable. The end of the bourgeois era was nowhere experienced so resplendently and so elegantly as in Vienna.

*Joachim C. Fest, 1973* [6b]

● Even as an adolescent Hitler had little affection either for Vienna or for the House of Habsburg. His aversion for Vienna, an aversion shared by a great many other Austrians, whether from Innsbruck, the Vorarlberg, Graz or elsewhere, would seem to have had its origins in Linz. But it was only after he had actually lived in the capital between 1908 and 1913 that he grew to hate it and to detest the Viennese dialect which, save for one or two idioms, he never used.

*Werner Maser, 1971* [17a]

## WAS HITLER REALLY POOR?

● I experienced such poverty in Vienna. I spent long months without ever having the smallest hot meal. I lived on milk and dry bread. But I spent thirty kreuzers a day on my cigarettes. I smoked between twenty-five and forty of them a day. Well, at that time a kreuzer meant more to me than ten thousand marks do to-day. One day I reflected that with five kreuzers I could buy some butter to put on my bread. I threw my cigarettes into the Danube, and since that day I've never smoked again.

*Hitler, March 11, 1942* [12b]

● Adolf's share of his father's inheritance produced a monthly income of 58 kronen, in addition to which he was receiving an orphan's pension of 25 kronen. With the large amounts also coming in from Walburga, (Hitler's legacy through his mother and his aunt Johanna Pölzl), he was thus very comfortably off. The rent he paid in Vienna amounted on average to some 10

14

Meldemannstrasse and ate at a convent. He did not drink, and gave up smoking, but as soon as he had a little money to spare, he hastened to gorge on cream puffs and other pastries.

Hitler had very few friends, although he knew many people of all kinds. Among them was a Jewish art buyer, Josef Neumann, who gave the penniless Hitler an overcoat. Another, Reinhold Hanisch, outlined a joint venture: Hitler would paint postcards and little pictures that Hanisch would then peddle. They would divide the proceeds evenly.

That scheme kept Hitler in pastries for a few months until Hanisch disappeared with the proceeds of a picture. Hitler re-

kronen a month.

At that time a lawyer's salary, after one year's practice in court, was 70 kronen a month, that of a teacher during the first five years of his career, 66 kronen.

*Werner Maser, 1971* [17b]

• Despite the expenses of her illness, his mother must have left her own two children at least 3,000 kronen, of which her golden boy probably received the larger part. In addition, as the orphaned children of a State official, they received during their minority or the period of their academic training an orphan's pension of 50 kronen monthly, of which sum Adolf for a time managed to obtain half by pretending to study at the Academy of Fine Arts—until his relatives discovered the swindle. So, to start with, by apportioning his capital Adolf Hitler could draw an unearned income of roughly 100 kronen a month—enough to live very decently. And if from the very beginning the young man felt the pinch from time to time that was solely because he went to the theatre every evening. . . .

*Helmut Heiber, 1960* [13b]

• [Hitler] still had some money left from his parental legacy, and he continued to receive his monthly allowance, but the uncertainty of his personal future nevertheless depressed him. He dressed carefully, still went to the opera, the theater, and the coffeehouses of the city; and, as he himself remarks, he continued, by careful speech and restrained bearing, to keep up his sense of bourgeois superiority to the working class. If we are to believe a somewhat dubious source on those years, he always carried with him an envelope of photographs showing his father in parade uniform and would smugly inform people that his late father had "retired as a higher official in his Imperial Majesty's Customs Service". . . .

. . . His principal fear was that the circumstances of the times might block his dream. He was afraid of an uneventful era. Even as a boy, he later declared, he had "indulged in angry thoughts concerning my earthly pilgrimage, which . . . had begun too late" and had "regarded the period 'of law and order' ahead . . . as a mean and undeserved trick of fate." This much he sensed: that only a chaotic fu-

"A View of the Karlskirche, Vienna," a pencil and watercolor painting by Adolf Hitler.

ported him to the police and Hanisch spent a week in jail.

Hitler had become a virtual drifter, but a drifter different from those with whom he shared flophouse dormitories and thin plates of bread-line soup. He would lie in his slovenly flat and dream up fantastic plots for getting rich and for changing the political system. From his experiences and observations of his grubby world, opinions were being shaped that were to become the cornerstone of his life.

Hitler read voraciously, but indiscriminately, in these years, borrowing regularly from the public library and spending endless hours browsing through book stores. Politics began to in-

---

ture and social upheaval could close the gap that separated him from reality. Wedded to his dreams, he was one of those who would prefer a life of disaster to a life of disillusionment.

*Joachim C. Fest, 1973* [6c]

• Hitler was happiest . . . among comrades whose principal subjects for discussion were schemes for making easy money. He found enthusiastic companions in Josef Greiner once a lamplighter, and an ex-priest named Grill. Together they dreamed up techniques for separating the public from its money, ranging from a hair restorer to a cream supposed to keep windows from breaking. The three young men spent their time continuously debating and arguing. Their attention wandered to other subjects—from politics and economics to astrology and the occult. Hitler always had a strong opinion and found ample opportunity for partisan debate.

*Bradley F. Smith, 1967* [32g]

## HITLER PAINTS AND STUDIES ARCHITECTURE

• He loved to pore through architecture books, memorizing pictures of the most famous buildings; then, with names covered, he tried to identify them. His reading was similarly playful and ranged over all subjects at random. He gathered tidbits of fact and opinion, seeking to confirm his biases rather than to build up any systematic knowledge of a subject.

He was always busy, dashing from one interest to another because of an "architect's" need to understand every part of human life in order to build properly. Nearly every day he journeyed around the city, "learning architecture" by looking at it. He loved to stand and gaze by the hour at monumental buildings. When he returned home he would pore over guidebooks in order to master more detail. From time to time, following these walks, he would explain to Kubizek the need to improve the housing of the masses. His

trigue him, and perhaps he had his first intimation that here lay the route to fame. He retained a handful of ideas that began to dominate him. He became convinced of the irretrievably evil nature of mankind and of the superiority of the Nordic Aryan race. He developed a deep distaste for democratic-parliamentary institutions and an implacable hatred of social democracy and Marxism.

He read simplified versions of the works of Friedrich Nietzsche, then Germany's most popular philosopher, with great interest; Hitler interpreted the author's message as a doctrine of the strong over the weak and the right of the sacred in-

concern, however, was restricted to the outward appearance of the city's districts; he displayed no sympathy for the housing problems of the common man. He did not like the Viennese people, finding them far too easygoing and frivolous, and he studiously avoided close contact with them. Although he suffered from Vienna's poor housing situation, he did not inquire into the actual living conditions of the people around him and felt no sense of comradeship with them.

*Bradley F. Smith, 1967* [32h]

● Hitler's drawings and paintings were not original, but copies, and Hanisch hawked them round the public houses in the evenings as the work of a sick or starving artist, thus finding buyers among the 'golden-hearted Viennese,' as indeed they were in those days. . . . Of the methods which Hanisch employed to sell his pictures Adolf, of course, had not the faintest idea and so believed they had market value as art.

*Franz Jetzinger, 1958* [15c]

## ADMIRATION FOR WAGNER

● . . . the Master of Bayreuth was not only Hitler's great exemplar; he was also the young man's ideological mentor. Wagner's political writings were Hitler's favorite reading, and the sprawling pomposity of his style unmistakably influenced Hitler's own grammar and syntax. Those political writings, together with the operas, form the entire framework for Hitler's ideology: Darwinism and anti-Semitism ("I hold the Jewish race to be the born enemy of pure humanity and everything noble in man"), the adoration of barbarism and Germanic might, the mystique of blood purification expressed in *Parzifal,* and the general histrionic view in which good and evil, purity and corruption, rulers and the ruled, stand opposed in black and white contrasts. The curse of gold, the inferior race grubbing underground, the conflict between Siegfried and Hagen, the tragic genius of Wotan—this strange brew compounded of bloody vapors, dragon slaying, mania for domination, treachery, sexuality, elitism, paganism, and ultimately

dividual to rule the vulgar masses.

He was particularly incensed at the Austrian parliament, which had men of various races among its members.

"The conviction grew in me," he said, "that this form of state could only bring disaster to the German nationality." He wanted Germans in parliament—pure, unadulterated Germans.

He began to get from his reading, his thinking, and Richard Wagner's music, on which he doted, a mystic concept of a Germany beleagured and divided by the machinations of Jewish radicals, and democrats in general.

Hitler's dislike of the Social Democrats developed when he

---

salvation and tolling bells on a theatrical Good Friday were the perfect ideological match for Hitler's anxieties and needs. Here he found the "granite foundations" for his view of the world.

*Joachim C. Fest, 1973* [6d]

I entered Wahnfried. To say I was moved is an understatement! At my worst moments, they've [the Wagner family] never ceased to sustain me, even Siegfried Wagner.

*Hitler, January 24, 1942* [12c]

● Wagner is responsible for the fact that the art of opera is what it is to-day. The great singers who've left names behind became celebrated as interpreters of Wagner. Moreover, it's since him that there have been great orchestra-leaders. Wagner was typically a prince. His house, Wahnfried, for example! It's been said that the interior, in Makart style, was overloaded. But should a house be mistaken for a gallery of works of art? Isn't it, above all, a dwelling, the framework for a private life, with its extensions and its radiance? . . .

. . . At the beginning of this century there were people called Wagnerians. Other people had no special name. What joy each of Wagner's works has given me! And I remember my emotion the first time

## CONTEMPT FOR NON-GERMANS

● Adolf's contempt for all the non-Germanic elements nourished by what he read, was realistically confirmed by the types with whom he constantly rubbed shoulders in the lodging houses—the human flotsam and jetsam that kept coming and going; the Slovak vagabond who emanated sickening stale odors of cheap alcohol; the consumptive Transylvanian whose continuous coughing and spitting would break up his sleep and frighteningly recall to him his similar illness a few years before; the old broken down Italian opera tenor, who except for his voice, would have remained a cobbler like his

came to believe that they were controlled by Jews. He was to write in *Mein Kampf* that this turned him from "a weakly cosmopolitan" into "a fanatical anti-Semite." Before he moved to Vienna, Hitler had regarded Jews merely as members of a different religion. "I was against the idea that he [the Jew] should be attacked because he had a different faith," he wrote. Now, in Vienna, where anti-Semitism was common, he was seeing the corrupt hand of Judaism everywhere.

"In my eyes the charge against Judaism became a grave one the moment I discovered the Jewish activities in the press, in art, in literature and the theatre," he wrote. At another point,

father before him; the filthy fox-eyed **Pole** so deep in slumber that **he was undis**turbed by the biting vermin that crawled over his bare back; the aged Hungarian nobleman who had squandered his entire inheritance in riotous living yet who gazed with patrician contempt at the young provincial whenever he began to harangue these and other lodgers with his trite speeches. It was the repulsive qualities of these "foreigners" with which Adolf invested their respective nationalities. Naturally he was blind to similar qualities in himself.

*Morris D. Waldman, 1962* [33a]

was a Jewish boy—"but we didn't give the matter any thought . . . I even took them [the Jews] for Germans."

According to Hitler's boyhood friend, this is not the truth. "When I first met Adolf Hitler," says August Kubizek, recalling their days together in Linz, "his anti-Semitism was already pronounced . . . Hitler was already a confirmed anti-Semite when he went to Vienna. And although his experiences in Vienna might have deepened this feeling, they certainly did not give birth to it."

*William L. Shirer, 1960* [24a]

## BECOMING AN ANTI-SEMITE

● . . . in Hitler's Vienna experience there were the Jews. In Linz, he says, there had been few Jews. "At home I do not remember having heard the word during my father's lifetime." At high school there

● Hostility to the Socialists and anti-Semitism were at that time the fashion among the ruling class in Vienna; they were "the right thing" in the bourgeois circles into which Hitler was trying to work his way. As an anti-Socialist and an anti-Semite one ranked among the better-class people. In parliament and, above all, in the Vienna Rathaus the clerical Christian-Socialist Party was politically predominant. This party, which was an in-

he asserted, "nine-tenths of all the smut literature, artistic trips, and theatrical banalities had to be charged to the Jews."

Like his anti-Semitism, Hitler's other attitudes and ideas were current in German circles at the time. Hitler embraced them with such enthusiasm and preached them with such animosity that he astounded and even frightened his daily companions who, perhaps for this reason, began to avoid him. Already could be seen the beginnings of the man who would mesmerize millions with his emotional oratory and illusory ideologies. A shy and unsure youth, his tongue loosened when the talk turned to politics, and he became frenziedly articulate.

veterate enemy of the Social Democrats and the Jews, was led by the burgomaster, Dr. Karl Lueger, the "most forceful German burgomaster of all time," as Hitler called him.

True, this forceful individual was a rather incomplete anti-Semite. For him a person who had been baptized was no longer a Jew; he was only opposed to the religion, not to the race. He persecuted Jews politically, but he associated with them in his private life. When someone lectured this autocratic man regarding one of his boon companions whose religious beliefs were suspect, he replied brutally: "As to whether a man's a Jew, that's for me to decide."

*Konrad Heiden, 1936* [10b]

• . . . since I had begun to concern myself with this question and to take cogni-

zance of the Jews, Vienna appeared to me in a different light than before. Wherever I went, I began to see Jews, and the more I saw, the more sharply they became distinguished in my eyes from the rest of humanity. Particularly the Inner City and the districts north of the Danube Canal swarmed with a people which even outwardly had lost all resemblance to Germans. . . .

. . . The cleanliness of this people, moral and otherwise, I must say, is a point in itself. By their very exterior you could tell that these were no lovers of water, and, to your distress, you often knew it with your eyes closed. Later I often grew sick to my stomach from the smell of these caftan-wearers. Added to this, there was their unclean dress and their generally unheroic appearance.

*Hitler, 1924* [11d]

# 2
# MUNICH AND WORLD WAR I

In May, 1913, Hitler moved to Munich, Germany, because he was about to be conscripted into the Austrian Army, and refused to serve "with filthy Czech Jews and the dregs of the Hapsburg monarchy." The new surroundings did not change his way of life; he found lodgings in a rundown section of the city and continued his makeshift life.

But for all his negative traits, Hitler was not a coward. When Germany declared war against France on August 3, 1914, he wrote to King Ludwig III of Bavaria asking permission to volunteer in the 16th Bavarian Reserve Infantry as an Austrian subject. Permission was granted. He later said he went down on his knees to thank Heaven he was alive to fight for Germany. Within two months, he was in the middle of the fighting.

From all accounts, Hitler was a good soldier, although he also had a reputation of being an annoying person and had few friends among the hard-bitten infantrymen. Frequently, he volunteered for dangerous duty, such as dispatch runner, which exposed him to enemy fire and shells. Once, he groveled at the feet of his colonel in a fit of zealous patriotism.

He saw his first combat action in the fierce fighting at Ypres, France, where his regiment was decimated. In 1915, he fought near Tourcoing and Neuve Chapelle, and the next year was in the bloody conflict at the Somme. In a battle near Bapaume, on October 7, 1916, he was wounded in the leg and hospitalized. During his convalescence he wrote to his colonel that he wanted to be recalled to duty as quickly as possible. "I do not want to be in Munich when my comrades are facing the enemy."

He returned to the front with the rank of corporal and fought in battle after battle. In one incident, he is said to have captured a group of French soldiers single-handedly. According to the legend, he encountered them in a shell hole and cowed them by pretending to have a platoon at his back. He was decorated with the Iron Cross, First Class, an exceptional honor for a cor-

Hitler (indicated by an "x" above his head) poses with other soldiers during World War I.

poral. The next October, once again at Ypres, his eyes were infected in a British gas attack and he collapsed. Once more, he was hospitalized. It was in a hospital bed, on November 11, 1918, that he learned the war was over. Germany had surrendered.

Hitler blamed the Jews for Germany's collapse. As he wrote, "was it all for this that the German soldier, exhausted by sleepless nights and endless marches, hungry, thirsty and frozen, had stood fast through burning sun and driving snow? Was it all for this, so that a mob of miserable criminals should dare to lay hands on the Fatherland?"

Hitler's reaction to what he considered the disgrace of Ger-

## HITLER GOES TO MUNICH

• He went to Munich in 1913 still chasing the will-o'-the-wisp of an artist's life. His dream of admission to the art academy in Munich failed to materialize, and he was forced to live by selling paintings as he had done in Vienna. However, in Munich he did not find a large commercial art market, and he was forced to hawk his pictures in beer halls and from door to door. Financially, the move to Munich was a failure and probably heightened his confusion about what he wanted to do with his life. It is not surprising, therefore, that he fell on his knees and thanked heaven when war came. The war provided him with an opportunity to realize his ideological dreams; more immediately, it also provided an escape from an increasingly serious economic dilemma.

*Bradley F. Smith, 1967* [321]

• In Munich Hitler's circumstances were as good as, if not better than, they had been in Vienna. It was not without reason that he later wrote: 'This period before the war was the happiest and by far the most contented of my life.' As a painter his average earnings amounted to the then considerable sum of a hundred marks a month. We know this from a letter he wrote to the Linz magistrates in reply to a summons issued after his repeated failure to report for military service. In that letter, dated January 1914, he enclosed a tax certificate in support of his statements.

*Werner Maser, 1971* [17c]

## ARMY DAYS

• Though he felt at home in the Army he could not refrain in the mess from holding forth on politics, especially indulging in his pet hatreds—for Marxists and Jews—in the excited manner of the old days of Vienna and more recently in Munich. Often he would sit in a corner with helmet on head buried deep in

many would have significance for his country and the rest of the world. "For my part, I then decided that I would take up political work." He had found a purpose in life and that, combined with his war experiences and deep anger over Germany's "betrayal," put an end to the ne'er-do-well idler of prewar days.

He rejoined his regiment on November 13 and was assigned to guard duty at a camp for Russian prisoners of war at Traunstein, east of Munich. Throughout Germany, there was chaos. In Munich, Kurt Eisner, a socialist, established and became president of the Republic of Bavaria, with the support of various people's councils. Kaiser Wilhelm II had abdicated his throne

thought, usually sullen and morose. But he never griped over Army food and stern discipline as did the others. This made them resentful, especially as he seemed to have been clever enough to avoid getting into the trenches.

*Morris D. Waldman, 1962* [33b]

● . . . he gave proof of his courage on many occasions. Though his comrades gave him credit for this, he struck them otherwise as a "queer card." He did not smoke, did not drink, had no thoughts about girls, hardly ever received a letter and never a parcel, and yet was overkeen as a soldier and at the slightest opportunity paraded extremist political views over which the others could only shake their heads. It was odd, to say the least, to hear this freak who usually converted his pay-packet into jam loosing off stilted phrases against the Jews or the Marxists, against affairs with French girls or against doubters in the victory of the German cause.

*Helmut Heiber, 1960* [13d]

## HE RECEIVES THE IRON CROSS

● . . . there is evidence to show that he was a comradely, level-headed and unusually brave soldier, and that a number of his commanding officers singled him out for special mention. Nevertheless political opponents at the time of the Weimar Republic put it about that he was not entitled to wear the Iron Cross 1st Class, a rumour which was revived after 1945. . . .

The National Socialists were themselves partly responsible for the unsavoury rumours that proliferated round Hitler's award of the Iron Cross 1st Class. They refused to admit (in so far as they knew) that the decoration Hitler proudly wore right up to the end of his life had been awarded him at the instance of a Jew—at the instance that is, of Hugo Gutmann, the regimental adjutant. Hitler had earned this recommendation after he had carried a message to the German artillery under exceptionally difficult conditions, and thus

two days before the armistice and fled the country. Socialists and Sparticists battled for control. The Sparticists, forerunners of the KPD (Communist Party), were hoping to transform Germany into a government along Soviet lines. Socialist democratic forces opposed the Sparticist movement, and bloody fighting shook the cities. The two chief Sparticist leaders were assassinated, and the situation calmed.

Meantime, the socialist-democratic government managed to retain control. With the support of the army, the people's councils were disbanded. In the elections of January 19, 1919, the socialists won by a slim margin; the rest of the votes were

prevented them from firing on their own infantry which in the meantime had taken up a more advanced position.

*Werner Maser, 1971* [17d]

### HITLER'S LETTERS

• Hitler's letters between 1905 and 1918 reveal a singular lack of warmth. They are obviously written by a person who pays heed to others only in so far as they can be of service to him and are prepared to act in accordance with criteria determined by him alone. He seldom asked after his correspondents' health save by way of conventional courtesies, nor did he ever seek their advice. He had no desire to enter into an exchange of ideas and regarded his own opinions as sacrosanct. All that he wanted, and indeed succeeded in finding, was a responsive audience prepared uncritically to accept his view of things.

*Werner Maser, 1971* [17e]

### HE LEARNS THE WAR HAS ENDED

• Since the day when I had stood at my mother's grave, I had not wept. When in my youth Fate seized me with merciless hardness, my defiance mounted. When in the long war years Death snatched so many a dear comrade and friend from our ranks, it would have seemed to me almost a sin to complain—after all, were they not dying for Germany? And when at length the creeping gas—in the last days of the dreadful struggle—attacked me, too, and began to gnaw at my eyes, and beneath the fear of going blind forever, I nearly lost heart for a moment, the voice of my conscience thundered at me: Miserable wretch, are you going to cry when thousands are a hundred times worse off than you! And so I bore my lot in dull silence. But now I could not help it. Only now did I see how all personal suffering vanishes in comparison with the misfortune of the fatherland. . . .

divided among the Catholic party, the Democrats, and the right-wing Nationalists. The spirit of the population was reflected in the grumbling about Germany's humiliation. Germany was stabbed in the back, the stories went. The invincible German army could never have been defeated by the inferior enemy forces had it not been for the betrayal by the enemy within: socialists, radical leftists, and Jews.

Hitler returned to Munich at the end of January. The city was still in an uproar, and the situation worsened in February, when Kurt Eisner, the Bavarian president, was assassinated. The political strife erupted into street violence. Hitler could see that his

. . . The more I tried to achieve clarity on the monstrous event in this hour, the more the shame of indignation and disgrace burned my brow. What was all the pain in my eyes compared to this misery?

There followed terrible days and even worse nights—I knew that all was lost. Only fools, liars, and criminals could hope in the mercy of the enemy. In these nights hatred grew in me, hatred for those responsible for this deed.

In the days that followed, my own fate became known to me. . . .

. . . I, for my part, decided to go into politics.

*Hitler, 1924* [11e]


### DEFEAT WAS INCONCEIVABLE


• The German people were dumbfounded and dismayed. They had, of course, suffered intolerable privations because of limited food, clothing and fuel.

Every family had sent one or more of its members to the fronts; many had been killed, many mutilated who, now at home, were an additional burden because of their helplessness. More, it was expected, would never return or, if alive, would come back crippled. But defeat had been inconceivable! The Army was regarded as invincible!

*Morris D. Waldman, 1962* [33c]

• Millions of Germans—perhaps the majority of Germans—never believed that the Allies achieved a military victory. Germany won nearly every battle from 1914 to 1918. As late as the offensive of March-to-May, 1918, General Paul von Hindenburg, the Kaiser's commander-in-chief, bent the Allied lines and penetrated perilously close to the French ports on the English Channel. On May 30, the Germans reached the Marne River again. The Allies started winning only in the second

fatherland was being torn to pieces. For a brief period, a social-democratic faction proclaimed the Red Republic of Bavaria. But the central government sent troops into Munich. They were joined by volunteer soldiers known as the "Freikorps." Soon a hungry, confused Munich surrendered to federal control.

In the Munich garrison, Hitler followed the turmoil in a depressed mood. He was 30 years old, his country was destroying itself, and he was a powerless corporal in a demoralized army. He was certain that the militant nationalism to which he was dedicated could solve his nation's problems. Do away with the pettifogging parliamentary government, the Jews, and the Bol-

---

fortnight of July, 1918, but the German war communiqués suppressed the truth until October, and the end came so quickly thereafter that few Germans could adjust their minds to the idea of Germany's defeat on the battlefield.

*Louis Fischer, 1941* [30a]

many at that time. It was the power of a falsehood, the poison of a propaganda which shrank from no distortion, from no untruth, over against which the German Reich stood virtually defenseless, because it was unprepared for it.

*Hitler, April 1, 1939* [22a]

## WHY DID GERMANY LOSE THE WAR?

• No 'stab in the back' had brought about the discomfiture of the German armies in the West. They were well and truly beaten in the field and they knew it.

*John W. Wheeler-Bennett, 1964* [29a]

• Germany at that time remained undefeated and unvanquished on land, at sea, and in the air. And yet we lost the war. We know the power which defeated Ger-

• To lose the War after having won almost all the battles was so startling and painful to patriots that they invented the "stab in the back" theory. The phantom backstabbers were the Socialists, Communists, Jews, democrats, and pacifists. They allegedly stabbed the nation in the back while the army still held the front. An unintelligent national pride made it seem pleasanter to succumb to the furtive hand of the internal foe than to the foreign mailed fist.

The authors of this myth obscured the simple truth that the last battle is decisive. They forgot that they had been hungry since 1916. Nations do not win wars on a diet of turnips and beets nor in half-paper suits that melt in the rain. Germany's man-

sheviks, and there would be a new, vital Germany.

He took a course in political instruction for soldiers and showed himself to be so astute that he was appointed a soldier-instructor. He was assigned to the investigative unit of the army "to gather evidence against those suspected of complicity with the Communists." Then he was told to infiltrate a new political group called the German Workers' Party. He could see immediately that it was not a radical leftist organization. There was only a handful of members; they had little capital, and their hatred was directed at the Jews and the Bolsheviks. He was intrigued.

power was exhausted. Germany's allies had crumpled. American troops had come into the War to help tip the balance against the Kaiser. But the militarists and reactionaries who had conducted the war wanted to evade the guilt of losing it.

*Louis Fischer, 1941* [30b]

first World War was lost, not through any merits of our enemies, but solely through our own fault.

*Hitler, January 30, 1942* [22b]

● The years 1914-1918 have proved one thing—our foes were not victorious. It was a despicable revolt, plotted by Marxist-Center-Liberalistic-Capitalist elements. The eternal Jew was the driving force behind them; it was they who caused Germany's downfall. Today, we know from English statements that in 1918 the English were facing their own collapse when —perhaps in the last quarter of the twelfth hour the German revolt at last materialized. This was aided by the cowardice of those governing Germany at the time, their indecision, vacillation and uncertainty. Thus it was possible that the

● The hidden forces which in 1914 incited England to the first World War, were Jews. The forces which then paralyzed us and finally forced us to surrender were Jewish. Jews instigated the Revolution, which robbed us of any possibility of further resistance. . . . When in November 1918 the German nation, dazed by the mendacious ideology of Wilson, President of the United States at the time, laid down its arms undefeated and left the battlefield, it did so under the influence of the Jewish race which hoped to erect a firm bulwark for the benefit of Bolshevism in the very heart of Europe.

*Hitler, April 26, 1942* [22c]

It was 1919, and an already embittered and confused German people suddenly were confronted with what was to become the Treaty of Versailles, a harsh treaty engineered by the Allies and used by the Nazis in later years to justify all manner of criminal behavior.

Under the terms of the treaty, Germany lost one-tenth of its European territory and population, including Alsace-Lorraine and the Saar coal fields. Germany lost three-quarters of its iron ore, one-quarter of its coal, and all its overseas territories. It might be noted that some of the territory lost had been gained in the previous century as a result of the Franco-Prussian War.

## HITLER IN 1919

• Neither parents nor brothers nor sisters, neither sweetheart nor friend awaited his return from the war. His sisters in Vienna did not even know where he was living. . . .

. . . he belonged to the so-called intelligence service, which is a discreet expression for espionage of any kind. At that time it was primarily a matter of political intelligence, by which must be understood not politics in the wide sense but the ferreting out of former partisans of the Soviet Government, who were to be shot. That was Adolf Hitler's business. And now we know what he had been during the Munich Soviet régime—a spy.

This occupation did not apparently inspire him with any horror. "There will be no peace in the land until a body is hanging from every lamp-post," he frequently remarked.

*Konrad Heiden, 1936* [10c]

• In 1919 at the latest his interest turned to literature of a pragmatic kind. Once he had taken up politics he regarded novels as a waste of time and poetry of any kind as superfluous, at least so far as he was concerned. The fields he eventually came to know best were those of architecture, art, military history, general history and technology; but he also felt at home in the spheres of music, biology, medicine, and the history of civilization and of religion. Indeed he was often able to surprise his listeners with his detailed and thorough knowledge of these subjects.

*Werner Maser, 1971* [17t]

## THE TREATY OF VERSAILLES

• A peace was established without regard for reality, indeed even without regard for the most primitive intelligence, a peace which was attended by a single

The treaty established the "Polish Corridor" to the sea and the free city of Danzig, both of which were to be sore points later. Almost as galling to the nationalistic militarist of Germany were the demilitarization of the Rhineland, rigid restrictions on the manufacture of war materials, and the reduction of the German navy to little better than a bathtub fleet.

Most important to the Germans, however, the Paris Peace Conference that devised the Versailles treaty placed the entire war guilt upon Germany and laid on a reparation indemnity of enormous proportions.

And so it was that when the Weimar constitution created a

---

thought: How can one suppress the vanquished, how can one deprive the defeated of all honor, how can one brand him for all eternity as the guilty one. It was a peace which was not peace, but which inevitably must lead to the perpetuation of hatred between nations.

*Hitler, October 24, 1933* [22d]

## A SHAMEFUL DICTATE

● The shameful dictate was intended to enslave the German nation forever. No limits had been set to this slavery. From the very outset they said: We will not state a definite sum for you to pay because we do not know what you are able to pay. From time to time we will fix new sums; but you must pledge yourselves immediately to pay everything we determine.

*Hitler, February 24, 1941* [22e]

## HITLER ATTENDS HIS FIRST GERMAN WORKER'S PARTY MEETING

● In the evening when I entered the 'Leiber Room' of the former Sterneckerbräu in Munich, I found some twenty to twenty-five people present, chiefly from the lower classes of the population.

[Gottfried] Feder's lecture was known to me from the courses, so I was able to devote myself to an inspection of the organization itself.

My impression was neither good nor bad; a new organization like so many others. This was a time in which anyone who was not satisfied with developments and no longer had any confidence in the existing parties felt called upon to found a new party. Everywhere these organizations sprang out of the ground, only to vanish silently after a time. The founders for the most part had no idea what it means to make a party—let alone a movement—out of a club. And so these organizations nearly always stifle automatically in their absurd philistinism.

federal republic in Germany on August 11, 1919, that republic, from its inception, presided over a people crippled in spirit and an economy that was shattered. It wasn't long before the term "November traitors" was used to refer to the leaders of the Weimar government, who were held responsible for carrying out the terms of the hated treaty.

Adolf Hitler was not crippled in spirit. He saw hopes for his soaring ambition in the lackluster German Workers' Party, which had been founded by Anton Drexler, a locksmith, and which confined its activities to debates and talks in beer halls. Here was the vehicle he could ride to power. From the moment

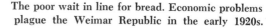

The poor wait in line for bread. Economic problems plague the Weimar Republic in the early 1920s.

he joined, he devoted all his energy to the party. He was placed in charge of propaganda, and soon hundreds of persons were attracted to party meetings.

In April, 1920, the future leader of the Nazi party left the army and devoted himself entirely to the workers' group. He ordered a change in its name to Nationalsozialistische Deutsche Arbeiterpartei or National Socialist German Workers' Party. (The first word of the German name was later abbreviated into Nazi.)

A wily propagandist, Hitler acquired a weekly newspaper, the *Völkischer Beobachter*, and began to spread his doctrine. He busied himself raising money and making ideological con-

---

I judged the 'German Workers' Party' no differently. When Feder finally stopped talking, I was happy. I had seen enough and wanted to leave when the free discussion period, which was now announced, moved me to remain, after all. But here, too, everything seemed to run along insignificantly until suddenly a 'professor' took the floor; he first questioned the soundness of Feder's arguments and then —after Feder replied very well—suddenly appealed to 'the facts,' but not without recommending most urgently that the young party take up the 'separation' of Bavaria from 'Prussia' as a particularly important programmatic point. With bold effrontery the man maintained that in this case German-Austria would at once join Bavaria, that the peace would then become much better, and more similar nonsense. At this point I could not help demanding the floor and giving the learned gentleman my opinion on this point—with the result that the previous speaker, even before I was finished, left the hall like a wet poodle. As I spoke, the audience had listened with astonished faces, and only as I was beginning to say good night to the assemblage

and go away did a man come leaping after me, introduce himself (I had not quite understood his name), and press a little booklet into my hand, apparently a political pamphlet, with the urgent request that I read it.

This was very agreeable to me, for now I had reason to hope that I might become acquainted with this dull organization in a simpler way, without having to attend any more such interesting meetings. Incidentally this apparent worker had made a good impression on me. And with this I left the hall.

*Hitler, 1924* [11f]

## FATHER OF THE FÜHRER LEGEND

● [The poet Dietrich Eckart] expounded his plans for the organization of the new party:

tacts with nationalistic movements and adherents in northern Germany. The former leaders of the Workers' Party began to realize that Hitler, more ambitious and overbearing with each passing month, had stolen their organization and was subverting it to his own uses. They tried to oust him, but they were no match for the wily Austrian. Hitler, the party's most powerful speaker, its best organizer, and its chief fund-raiser, threatened to resign. The leaders capitulated, and acceded to Hitler's demand that the party statutes be amended so that all power would be concentrated in the hands of the party chairman, who, of course, was Adolf Hitler.

"We must have a fellow at the head who won't wince at the rattle of a machine-gun. The rabble must be given a damned good fright. An officer wouldn't do; the people don't respect them any more. Best of all would be a workman in a soldier's coat and with his tongue in the right place. Good Lord, if Noske weren't such a—" another strong expression. "He needn't be very brainy; politics is the most imbecile business in the world and every market-woman in Munich knows as much as those fellows in Weimar. I'd rather have a stupid, vain jackanapes who can give the Reds a juicy answer and not run away whenever a chair-leg is aimed at him than a dozen learned professors who sit trembling on the wet trousers-seat of facts."

And as a crowning piece of wisdom he announced: "He must be a bachelor! Then we shall get the women."

A number of people still living can recall this prophetic picture which Dietrich Eckart sketched of Adolf Hitler in a Schwabing wine-room. Eckart was the spiritual father of the *Führer* legend in the National-Socialist Party.

*Konrad Heiden, 1936* [10d]

### HITLER'S FIRST POLITICAL FOOTSTEPS

• Anyone acquainted with the unhappy life of this lonely man [Hitler] knows why hatred and persecution mania guided his first political footsteps. In his heart he nursed a grudge against the world, and he vented it on guilty and innocent alike. His croaking voice, his jerky gait, his sawing gestures expressed a hatred of which all who saw him were conscious.

*Konrad Heiden, 1936* [10e]

• I knew what these men felt: it was the longing for a new movement which should be more than a party in the previous sense of the word. . . .

. . . This absurd little organization with its few members seemed to me to possess the one advantage that it had not frozen into an 'organization,' but left the individual an opportunity for real personal activity. Here it was still possible to work,

Munich in these restless postwar years was surging with groups such as the Workers' Party, all aimed at rescuing their country from the shame wrought by defeat and the hated Versailles treaty. Ex-officers and soldiers filled the beer halls of the city with talk of overthrowing the German Republic through a military resurgence. Among these the Workers' Party and Hitler were emerging as key figures.

Why Hitler, why this man, whose moods shifted from bleak depression to soaring elation with blurring rapidity, this rejected artist from a small town in Austria? First, he spoke of solutions, of German pride, of hatred, to people who were

and the smaller the movement, the more readily it could be put into the proper form. Here the content, the goal, and the road could still be determined, which in the existing great parties was impossible from the outset.

The longer I tried to think it over, the more the conviction grew in me that through just such a little movement the rise of the nation could some day be organized, but never through the political parliamentary parties which clung far too greatly to the old conceptions or even shared in the profits of the new régime. For it was a new philosophy and not a new election slogan that had to be proclaimed.

*Hitler, 1924* [11g]

### OPPOSITION IN THE PARTY

• It grows more and more clear that his purpose is simply to use the National Socialist Party as a springboard for his own immoral purposes, and to seize the leadership in order to force the Party on to a different track at the psychological moment. This is most clearly shown by an ultimatum which he sent to the Party leaders a few days ago, in which he demands amongst other things that he shall have a sole and absolute dictatorship of the Party, and that the Committee, including the locksmith Anton Drexler, the founder and leader of the Party, should retire. . . .

. . . A further point is the question of his occupation and finances. If ever individual members inquire what he actually lives on and what his previous occupation has been, he always gets excited and loses his temper. . . .

. . . And how does he carry on his campaign? Like a Jew. He twists every fact and makes out that Drexler is not sufficiently revolutionary and that he wants to return to the parliamentary system. What are the real facts? Drexler has never budged an inch from the standpoint that he occupied when he first founded the Party.

*From a leaflet circulated*
*among members of the*
*National Socialist Party, 1921* [9a]

aching with discontent, and he backed up his opinions with "facts" culled from his vast reading, even though those facts may have been only half digested.

But mainly his strength lay in the power of his speechmaking. Janet Flanner, the writer who has been observing the European scene for decades, described him as a "born spellbinder, who produces in crowds the excitement he produces in himself. His oratorical powers were the basis of his career."

Soon, the paramilitary aspect of the party became apparent. Hitler created a "gymnastic-sports" division, and goon squads calling themselves Sturm-Abteilung (assault troops), or SA, be-

**HITLER SPEAKS TO YOUNG NAZIS**

• The Marxists taught: If you will not be my brother, I will bash your skull in. Our motto shall be: If you will not be a German, I will bash your skull in. For we are convinced that our Movement cannot succeed without a struggle. We have to fight with ideas, but if necessary also with our fists. I remind you of the 2,000,000 dead on the fields of battle. They are asking of you an infinitely smaller sacrifice than they made themselves. Our enemies realize that the future of our people depends on you. Young Germany—that is what you are. And that is why they hate you. Be proud that they hate you, obstinately proud. Hail to you!

*Hitler, November 1922* [22f]

**THE SA**

• Except for a generalized nationalistic belligerence, the SA did not develop any distinctive ideology (contrary to what many participants have said in their reminiscences). When it paraded through the streets under waving banners, it was certainly not marching toward a new social order. It had no utopian ideas, merely an enormous restiveness; no goal but dynamic energy, which often ran out of control. Strictly speaking, most of those who joined its columns were not even political soldiers. Rather, their temper was that of mercenaries, and the high-sounding political phrases were only a cloak for their nihilism, their restlessness, and their craving for something to which they could subordinate themselves. Their ideology was action at all costs. In keeping with the spirit of male comradeship and homosexuality that permeated the SA, the average storm trooper gave his allegiance not to a program, but to an individual, "a leader personality." Hitler, in fact, wanted it so. In a proclamation he had stipulated: "Let only those apply who wish to be obedient to the leaders and are prepared, if need be, to meet death."

*Joachim C. Fest, 1973* [6e]

gan raiding communist meetings at beer halls. This Brown Shirt militia was eventually to expand to 800,000 men.

By the early 1920s, the party was organized into a well-knit, compact structure based on the Leader Principle (Führerprinzip). The authority of the leader was absolute. Under him, the higher-ranking executives were linked to the Führer by direct, personal responsibility and exercised a certain autonomy of action. Military forces were all subject to the party's hierarchy. Hitler left little room for the formation and development of ideological debate. Any difference of opinion was stifled immediately by force, a policy that was to be one of the most heinous features

## HITLER ATTENDS A PARTY

● Hitler . . . displayed a certain crude talent for thrusting himself into the limelight, which, though not very attractive, was highly effectual. One of Hitler's fellow-guests at a party in the year 1923 writes as follows:

"We were all very excited, because we knew that Herr Hitler was coming. Very few of us had heard him speak at a meeting or seen him at close quarters, but, on the other hand everyone had heard and read a great deal about him. The simple folk of Munich idolized him and even some of the more discriminating found him interesting. He had sent word to the hostess that he had to attend an important meeting and so would not arrive until late: I think it was about eleven o'clock. He came, none the less, in a very decent blue suit and with an extravagantly large bouquet of roses, which he presented to his hostess as he kissed her hand. While he was being introduced, he wore the expression of a public prosecutor at an execu-

tion. I remember being struck by his voice when he thanked the lady of the house for tea or cakes, of which, incidentally, he ate an amazing quantity. It was a remarkably emotional voice, and yet it made no impression of cordiality or intimacy but rather of harshness. However, he said hardly anything but sat there in silence for about an hour; apparently he was tired. Not until the hostess was so incautious as to let fall a remark about the Jews, whom she defended in a jesting tone, did he begin to speak, and then he spoke without ceasing. After a while he thrust back his chair and stood up, still speaking or rather yelling, in such a powerful penetrating voice as I have never heard from anyone else. In the next room a child woke up and began to cry. After he had for more than half an hour delivered a quite witty but very one-sided oration on the Jews, he suddenly broke off, went up to the hostess, begged to be excused, and kissed her hand again as he took his leave. The rest of the company, who apparently had not pleased him, were only vouchsafed a curt bow from the doorway."

*Konrad Heiden, 1936* [10]

of the Third Reich.

Given Hitler's extremism, his irrational, complex, and contradictory character, historians always have marveled at his ability to attract the loyal following of men who were his social and intellectual superiors. But Germany was fast slipping into deep economic and political despair, and the need for a leader with strong beliefs was desperate. At any rate, the hierarchy of the party was illuminating. Around Hitler in the executive cadre were such men as Dietrich Eckart, a journalist, playwright, and poet, who traveled in high society; Ernst Röhm, an army major with a reputation as a brilliant organizer and skilled collector

## WHERE DID HITLER GET HIS MONEY?

● . . . in December of 1920, the party had acquired a run-down newspaper badly in debt, the *Voelkischer Beobachter,* an anti-Semitic gossip sheet which appeared twice a week. Exactly where the sixty thousand marks for its purchase came from was a secret which Hitler kept well, but it is known that Eckart and Roehm persuaded Major General Ritter von Epp, Roehm's commanding officer in the Reichswehr and himself a member of the party, to raise the sum. Most likely it came from Army secret funds.

*William L. Shirer, 1960* [24b]

● Two years after the *Völkischer Beobachter* had been bought for him, Hitler made it into a daily. This required money. Some of it was provided by Frau Gertrud von Seidlitz, a Baltic lady who had shares in Finnish paper mills, while Putzi Hanf-

stängl, a son of the rich Munich family of art publishers, advanced a loan of a thousand dollars. Hanfstängl, who had been educated at Harvard, not only took Hitler into his own home—where he delighted him by his piano-playing, especially of Wagner—but introduced him to a number of other well-to-do Munich families, including the Bruckmanns, another firm of Munich publishers.

*Alan Bullock, 1962* [4a]

● In his memoirs, *Unheard Witness,* Hanfstaengl says that he was first steered to Hitler by an American. This was Captain Truman Smith, then an assistant military attaché at the American Embassy in Berlin. In November 1922 Smith was sent by the embassy to Munich to check on an obscure political agitator by the name of Adolf Hitler and his newly founded National Socialist Labor Party. For a young professional American Army officer, Captain Smith had a remarkable bent for political analysis. In one week in Munich, November 15–22, he managed to see Lu-

of financial contributions from military quarters; Gottfried Feder, an engineer and dilettante socialist-economist; Alfred Rosenberg, an Estonian who escaped from Moscow during the Bolshevik Revolution and who became the party's tireless, hairsplitting theorist on the principles of race and Aryan culture; and Nuremberg Jew-baiter Julius Streicher, an elementary schoolmaster and founder-editor of *Der Sturmer*, the most obscenely anti-Semitic journal in Germany.

A prize catch was General Erich Ludendorff, former chief of Field Marshal Paul von Hindenburg's Imperial General Staff. The old fire-eating Prussian made fine window-dressing, but

L-R: Gen. Erich Ludendorff, Adolf Hitler, Wilhelm Brückner, and Ernst Röhm in 1923.

dendorff, Crown Prince Rupprecht and a dozen political leaders in Bavaria, most of whom told him that Hitler was a rising star and his movement a rapidly growing political force. Smith lost no time in attending an outdoor Nazi rally at which Hitler spoke. "Never saw such a sight in my life!" he scribbled in his diary immediately afterward. "Met Hitler," he wrote, "and he promises to talk to me Monday and explain his aims." On the Monday, Smith made his way to Hitler's residence—"a little bare bedroom on the second floor of a run-down house," as he described it— and had a long talk with the future dictator, who was scarcely known outside Munich. "A marvelous demagogue!" the assistant U.S. military attaché began his diary that evening. "Have rarely listened to such a logical and fanatical man." The date was November 22, 1922.

*William L. Shirer, 1960* [24c]

## MONEY FROM ABROAD

● At the height of the year 1923 it was the chaos which literally fed him and his

little else. He is generally supposed to have become deranged about this time.

The figure who was to become the best known to the public was no less accomplished: Captain Hermann Goering, World War I ace of famed Baron Manfred von Richthofen's Flying Service and its leader after the Baron was shot down. He took over as leader of the Brown Shirts.

Basically, however, party membership consisted of rootless ex-soldiers who, in the formation of activist units such as the SA, found the outlets for which they longed. The middle class, while slow to join such a roughneck group, admired the party's

followers; for the decay of the mark blew small financial contributions, made in substantial foreign currency by friends in Czechoslovakia, Switzerland, the United States, up to gigantic sums in marks; a person could live comfortably for a week on a dollar at that time, and for a hundred dollars one could buy a minor revolution. It was a decisive turn in Hitler's career when his friend and admirer, Ernst Hanfstaengl, scion of an old-established, wealthy printer's family, himself half-American by descent, borrowed for him the fabulous sum of one thousand dollars. This money enabled Hitler to set up, in February, 1923, the *Völkischer Beobachter* as a daily paper.

*Konrad Heiden, 1944* [8a]

● That Henry Ford, the famous automobile-manufacturer, gave money to the National Socialists, directly or indirectly, has never been disputed. Ford is an anti-Semite, and a National-Socialist agent, Lüdecke by name, made a journey to America in 1925 in order to get money from him.

One abundant source of money was Switzerland. In 1923 a certain Dr. Emil Gansser toured that country, canvassing, in particular, wealthy Swiss Protestants. To an evangelical mission inspector in Switzerland Gansser wrote on April 2, 1922, from Munich: "I observed with keen delight on my last journey through Switzerland that among the influential German families Hitler's great ideological struggle is followed with far more attention and sympathy than in my own country...."

*Konrad Heiden, 1936* [10a]

## ATTRACTING THE MASSES

● To whom should propaganda be addressed? To the scientifically trained intelligentsia or to the less educated masses?

... The function of propaganda does not lie in the scientific training of the individual, but in calling the masses' attention to certain facts, processes, necessities, etc., whose significance is thus for the first time placed within their field of vision.

The whole art consists in doing this so skillfully that everyone will be convinced

objectives. Small merchants, particularly, felt oppressed by big business. Now, impoverished by the economic crisis, they were dazzled at the prospect of attacking the large department stores owned by Jews.

These and others of the petite bourgeoisie formed the foundation of Hitler's power. After suffering through the rigors of war, they had found themselves with nothing to show for their sacrifices. Here, at least, was a man who promised to help them if he could control the instruments of power. What if he did seem outrageous, even unstable at times? He vowed to regenerate Germany, and that was their dearest dream.

---

that the fact is real, the process necessary, the necessity correct, etc. But since propaganda is not and cannot be the necessity in itself, since its function, like the poster, consists in attracting the attention of the crowd, and not in educating those who are already educated or who are striving after education and knowledge, its effect for the most part must be aimed at the emotions and only to a very limited degree at the so-called intellect. . . .

. . . But the most brilliant propagandist technique will yield no success unless one fundamental principle is borne in mind constantly and with unflagging attention. It must confine itself to a few points and repeat them over and over. Here, as so often in this world, persistence is the first and most important requirement for success.

*Hitler, 1924* [11h]

● The first years of my struggle were therefore concentrated on the object: win over the worker to the National-Socialist Party. Here's how I set about it:

1. I followed the example of the Marxist parties by putting up posters in the most striking red.

2. I used propaganda trucks that were literally carpeted with posters of a flaming red, equipped with equally red flags and occupied by thundering loud-speakers.

3. I saw to it that all the initiates of the movement came to meetings without stiff collars and without ties, adopting the free-and-easy style so as to get the workers into their confidence.

4. As for the bourgeois elements who, without being real fanatics, wanted to join the ranks of the National-Socialist Party, I did everything to put them off—resorting to bawled-out propaganda, dishevelled clothes, etc. My object was to rid myself right from the beginning of the revolutionaries in rabbits' pelts.

5. I ordered our protective service to treat our opponents roughly and chuck them out of our meetings with so little mildness that the enemy press—which otherwise would have ignored our gatherings—used to make much of the blows and wounds they give rise to, and thus called attention to them.

*Hitler, April 8, 1942* [12d]

# 3

# THE BEER HALL PUTSCH PRISON, AND MEIN KAMPF

The year 1923 was a decisive and dramatic one for Germany and Adolf Hitler. Monetary inflation soared dizzily. The German mark, which at the end of the war was valued at four to the American dollar, skidded to a ratio of 7,000 to the dollar by early 1923. Negotiations for payment of war damages to the Western Allies came to a standstill. In retaliation, France sent a military occupation force into the Ruhr, the heart of industrial Germany. For proud Germans, the act was the ultimate humiliation by a despised neighbor.

To Hitler, the time seemed right for bold action. He had been greatly impressed by the success of Benito Mussolini's march on Rome the year before. For months he had been planning a similar march on Germany's capital, Berlin, with the intention of overthrowing the government of the "November traitors." But he needed to solidify his support in Bavaria first, and in that state the crosscurrents of politics were complicated indeed. The government was headed by Gustav von Kahr, who wanted to see the monarchy restored. Neither he nor Bavaria's army commandant, General Otto von Lossow, made a secret of the fact that they did not recognize the authority of the central government. Both men, however, regarded the corporal-turned-demagogue with some disdain.

Hitler selected a rash approach to further his schemes. On November 8, high-ranking Bavarian generals, ministers, government officials, and politicians assembled for a rally in the beer hall of the Munich city hall. This was the setting for what has become known as the Munich putsch, or small rebellion. When the SA troops stormed into the auditorium and Hitler made his way to the platform, Commissioner von Kahr was addressing the gathering. Outside, other members of the Brown Shirts set up machine-gun implacements. Hitler raised a pistol over his head, fired two shots in the air, and announced that his squadrons had taken over the city.

## INFLATION AND ITS EFFECTS

• The occupation of the Ruhr gave the final touch to the deterioration of the mark. By 1 July 1923 the rate of exchange with the dollar had risen to a hundred and sixty thousand marks; by 1 August to a million; by 1 November to a hundred and thirty thousand million. The collapse of the currency not only meant the end of trade, bankrupt businesses, food shortage in the big cities and unemployment: it had the effect, which is the unique quality of economic catastrophe, of reaching down to and touching every single member of the community in a way which no political event can. The savings of the middle classes and working classes were wiped out at a single blow with a ruthlessness which no revolution could ever equal; at the same time the purchasing power of wages was reduced to nothing. Even if a man worked till he dropped it was impossible to buy enough clothes for his family—and work, in any case, was not to be found.

*Alan Bullock, 1962* [41]

• From then on [1921], goaded by the big industrialists and landlords, who stood to gain though the masses of the people were financially ruined, the government deliberately let the mark tumble in order to free the State of its public debts, to escape from paying reparations and to sabotage the French in the Ruhr. Moreover, the destruction of the currency enabled German heavy industry to wipe out its indebtedness by refunding its obligations in worthless marks. The General Staff, disguised as the "Truppenamt" (Office of Troops) to evade the peace treaty which supposedly had outlawed it, took notice that the fall of the mark wiped out the war debts and thus left Germany financially unencumbered for a new war.

The masses of the people, however, did not realize how much the industrial tycoons, the Army and the State were benefiting from the ruin of the currency. All they knew was that a large bank account could not buy a straggly bunch of carrots, a half peck of potatoes, a few ounces of sugar, a pound of flour. They knew that as individuals they were bankrupt. And they knew hunger when it gnawed at

He herded von Kahr, von Lossow, and the chief of police into a small adjoining room. He demanded their cooperation with his plans. The three men would not agree initially, then appeared to go along with him.

After the meeting, the city government officials quickly learned that Hitler's forces did not control Munich. Only Röhm's squadron had taken action and occupied the general-staff headquarters of the army. The officials were free to put down this upstart's plans. They immediately informed the government in Berlin of the day's events and, during the night, government troops were placed in strategic areas of the city.

them, as it did daily. In their misery and hopelessness they made the Republic the scapegoat for all that had happened.

        *William L. Shirer, 1960* [24d]

● Believe me, our misery will increase. The scoundrel will get by. But the decent, solid businessman who doesn't speculate will be utterly crushed; first the little fellow on the bottom, but in the end the big fellow on top too. But the scoundrel and the swindler will remain, top and bottom. The reason: because the state itself has become the biggest swindler and crook. A robbers' state! . . .

        *Hitler, quoted by Konrad Heiden* [8b]

## ON A COLLISION COURSE

● As the police warned the government at the beginning of 1923, Hitler was sailing a collision course with the authorities.

He preached revolution and clearly believed his own propaganda. This meant that, as long as the "system" he hated existed, he could be expected to take action against it as soon as he felt strong enough to do so. In turn, Hitler's propaganda had a terrific impact on his followers. Even had he not believed in the proposals he made and the revolution he promised, the mass of his followers did believe. This meant that sooner or later, he would be forced to revolt or lose them.

        *Harold J. Gordon, Jr., 1972* [31a]

## THE NSDAP AS CATALYST

● In many ways, the NSDAP was the most important single element in the political spectrum in Bavaria in 1923. It was important less because of its size and power than because of its nature and potential. Most of all, it was important because it was a catalyst that brought a com-

The next day, November 9, several thousand party members tramped toward the center of Munich. Hitler led the march, the revered General Ludendorff beside him. Hitler knew that no one would dare shoot at this national hero. Many soldiers and officers, seeing the dignified old general, drew to attention and seemed ready to follow him to Berlin, if asked.

In the narrow Residenzstrasse, the parade encountered a police cordon. Ordered to halt, the defiant mob still moved forward. Shots rang out. Three policemen and 16 Nazis were killed. Thousands of other Nazis scattered wildly. But General Ludendorff fearlessly marched ahead and was arrested by

paratively stable system into violent if brief motion and both rationalized and polarized the political positions of individuals and groups.

*Harold J. Gordon, Jr., 1972* [31b]

## THE BEER HALL PUTSCH

• [Hitler] had never planned a revolutionary take-over in Munich; rather, he had intended to march against Berlin, with Munich's might behind him. . . .

. . . the prospects for a "March on Berlin" were by no means unfavorable. As became clear the next morning [November 9], public sentiment was clearly on the side of Hitler and the Kampfbund. From numerous apartment house windows and even from City Hall and public buildings

Hitler and his Nazi comrades march through the streets of Munich in 1923, as watching Germans salute them.

police. Hitler, on the other hand, flung himself to the ground so hastily that he injured his shoulder. According to testimony in the trial later, the future leader of the Third Reich was among the first to pick himself up and run for cover. He escaped, but was captured later in the country cottage of a friend.

The Munich beerhall putsch trial began in February, 1924, and lasted for 24 days. Correspondents from all over Germany and elsewhere covered the proceedings, because it appeared that Hitler was becoming a German of national stature. However, the fiasco of Munich seemed certain to destroy any claims he might have had to national leadership. The judge decided

that Hitler was not a danger and did not press for severe punishment. In fact, he was sentenced to five years in prison, but with the understanding that he would receive an early pardon.

The Landsberg prison to which he was sent was more like a first-class hotel than a penitentiary for Hitler and the 40 other Nazis confined with him. Certainly, bars protected the windows, but the cells were big and airy. Doors were left open. Hitler's group had a living room and was allowed to spend many hours walking in the garden.

Hitler read, gained weight, talked with a retinue of visitors, gave lengthy interviews to the press. He began to dictate his

---

the swastika flag fluttered, and the newspaper accounts of the events in the Bürgerbräukeller had an approving tone. Many people came to the campaign headquarters the Kampfbund had set up in various parts of the city, while in the barracks the lower rank officers and the enlisted men frankly expressed their sympathy with Hitler's plans for the march. The speakers whom Streicher had sent around were met with hearty applause in the strangely feverish atmosphere of that bleak November morning.

*Joachim C. Fest, 1973* [6f]

fact remains that according to the testimony of one of his own Nazi followers in the column, the physician Dr. Walther Schulz, which was supported by several other witnesses, Hitler "was the first to get up and turn back," leaving his dead and wounded comrades lying in the street. He was hustled into a waiting motorcar and spirited off to the country home of the Hanfstaengls at Uffing, where Putzi's wife and sister nursed him and where, two days later, he was arrested.

*William L. Shirer, 1960* [24e]

● The future Chancellor of the Third Reich was the first to scamper to safety. He had locked his left arm with the right arm of Scheubner-Richter (a curious but perhaps revealing gesture) as the column approached the police cordon, and when the latter fell he pulled Hitler down to the pavement with him. Perhaps Hitler thought he had been wounded; he suffered sharp pains which, it was found later, came from a dislocated shoulder. But the

**FOURTEEN MARTYRS**

● . . . fourteen Putschists, who were later immortalized as martyrs of the movement, were slain. They were a cross-section of the Putschists—rich and poor, educated

political creed, *Mein Kampf* (My Struggle), to Emil Maurice and, later, to Rudolf Hess, who acted as Hitler's secretaries during their imprisonment. A former pilot in the German Air Force, Hess was a strange, fanatical-looking man with piercing eyes and thick eyebrows. He was a devotee of astrology and Nordic mythology. Primarily, though, he was "devoted" to Hitler.

*Mein Kampf*, first published in 1925, became a world-wide best-seller and eventually made Hitler a millionaire. It is an unparalleled document of hatred, cynicism, and arrogance. In it, Hitler blueprinted each step of aggression he planned and was to execute some 15 years later. Germany, he wrote, was fated

and ignorant, worker and noble, leader and follower—but the bulk of them, like the bulk of the National Socialists, were young. Although a high percentage of those killed were leaders of the party, of the sixteen men slain in both encounters only five were over thirty years of age and nine were below twenty-six. Some of them were men whose loss may well have been significant; others were men who could have done nothing as valuable for the party in life as they did in dying for it. They became the kernel of a myth that played a significant part in bringing the party to power. Through them, ignominious failure was made into glorious defiance of tryranny.

*Harold J. Gordon, Jr., 1972* [31c]

• . . . Ludendorff showed merely foolhardiness, pride, or confidence in his destiny. I have never heard a man who had been in combat criticize Hitler for dropping, but many have criticized Ludendorff

for not doing so. After all, only if you fall down do you have a chance to fight back effectively.

*Harold J. Gordon, Jr., 1972* [31d]

## HIS SECOND CRISIS

• The Putsch had transformed the old Hitler into the new, just as World War I and the revolution had turned the bohemian would-be artist of Vienna and München into a revolutionary leader—and of the two transformations it was perhaps the greater. Hitler's first crisis had made him a revolutionary. His second made him the undisputed leader of a serious political movement. The third crisis brought him to the helm of Germany, while the fourth led him to conquest, defeat, and death. In 1925 he was therefore at the halfway point of his political career, although most Germans who had heard of him at that time would have guessed that his career was behind him.

*Harold J. Gordon, Jr., 1972* [31e]

to conquer, and he was to be its conquering leader. His plan to liquidate the Jewish peoples was detailed in full. He even described propaganda techniques that an unscrupulous ruler could use to gain his own ends. The big lie repeated often enough becomes believable—and the bigger the lie, the better the propaganda value. Tolerance of anyone else's viewpoint was unthinkable. "What would you think of an advertisement for soap which stated that other soaps were also good?" he wrote.

Outside the prison, meantime, his Nazi party was dissolving. The government had banned it, and its leadership scattered in diverse directions. Ludendorff came to an agreement with the

### THE TRIAL

• Many times in the course of the trial [Hitler] was asked directly and indirectly by what right he, a man without origins, title, or virtually any education, arrogated to himself the right to govern Germany, sweeping aside all the generals, presidents, and excellencies. Hitler replied: 'This was not overweening or immodest of me. On the contrary, I am of the opinion that when a man knows he can do a thing, he has no right to be modest. . . .

. . . 'My standpoint is that the bird must sing because he is a bird. And a man who is born for politics must engage in politics whether at freedom or in prison, whether he sits in a silken chair or must content himself with a hard bench. . . . The man who is born to be a dictator is not compelled; he wills; he is not driven forward; he drives himself forward; there is nothing immodest about this. Is it immodest for a worker to drive himself toward heavy labor? Is it presumptuous of a man with the high forehead of a thinker to ponder through the nights till he gives the world an invention? The man who feels called upon to govern a people has no right to say: If you want me or summon me, I will co-operate. No, it is his duty to step forward. . . .'

*Hitler, at the trial, 1924* [8c]

• Hitler was shrewd enough to see that his trial, far from finishing him, would provide a new platform from which he could not only discredit the compromised authorities who had arrested him but—and this was more important—for the first time make his name known far beyond the confines of Bavaria and indeed of Germany itself.

*William L. Shirer, 1960* [24f]

• I believe that the hour will come when the masses, who today stand on the street with our swastika banner, will unite with those who fired upon them.

*Hitler, at the trial, 1924* [8d]

northern nationalists and, in the spring elections that year, their united front collected a million votes and 32 seats in the German parliament, the Reichstag. Streicher founded a new party, Union of the Greater Germany, based on the fundamental tenets of the Nazi party. Röhm, always militaristically oriented, organized his own version of the Brown Shirts, the Frontbann.

When Hitler was granted a qualified release on Christmas Eve, 1924, he was confronted with two problems: how to reconstruct the movement under his own aegis and how to regain political credibility after the aborted November putsch. Actually, he was not bothered that the party had been dissolved while

● . . . there can be no doubt that the same terrible sincerity spoke here that would speak again and again in the future. Hitler did not feel himself to be a criminal in 1924, and he did not feel himself to be a criminal in 1945. He was the archetype of the "true believer," and his belief was in himself and his heaven-ordained mission. As least in part, it was the terrible sincerity within him that reached out and held his listeners in thrall.

*Harold J. Gordon, Jr., 1972* [31f]

### A MILD SENTENCE

● *Hitler:* '. . . You may pronounce us guilty a thousand times over, the goddess of the eternal court of history will smile and tear to tatters the brief of the state's attorney and the sentence of the court; for she acquits us.'

The sentence of the judges was not so far from the judgment of history. Intimi-dated from above, tormented by the conscience of their own accomplices, in fear even of the accused, they trampled on what was most defenseless: justice. Contrary to the clear wording of the law, Ludendorff was totally acquitted. Contrary to the clear wording of the law, Hitler, despite the bloody consequences of his crime, received the mild minimum sentence of five years' imprisonment; contrary to the clear wording of the law, he was made to serve only eight and a half months of his term; contrary to the clear wording of the law, he, a foreigner, who had filled the German streets with fire and corpses, was not deported. Röhm and Frick, though formally condemned, were released at once. Göring had fled to Italy and later went to his wife's native Sweden. His unfounded fear of Munich justice kept him for nearly three years in unnecessary exile. Hess was cleverer; he returned, and an equally mild and brief sentence brought him to the same so-called 'prison' as Hitler, a sanatorium-like building in the little city of Landsberg am Lech.

*Konrad Heiden, 1944* [8o]

he was in prison; it meant that no one could replace him as leader. His first move was to get the government to cancel the ban on his party. Less than two weeks after his release, he conferred with the Bavarian prime minister. Abjectly admitting all past mistakes and vowing that the one purpose of his party was to fight Marxism and Judaism, he persuaded the minister to rescind the ban. A few months later, the government relaxed further by permitting Hitler once more to make public speeches. Immediately, Hitler and his aides arranged for a huge rally of the faithful to demonstrate to the world that he remained the leader of a viable party and to prevent any backsliding among

• When the lay judges protested at the severity of the sentence, the President of the Court assured them that Hitler would certainly be pardoned and released on probation. Despite the objection of the State Prosecutor and the attempts of the police to get him deported, Hitler was in fact released from prison after serving less than nine months of his sentence—and promptly resumed his agitation against the Republic. Such were the penalties of high treason in a State where disloyalty to the régime was the surest recommendation to mercy.

*Alan Bullock, 1962* [4b]

• One can criticize the verdict point by point. The crime is evident: its authors intended to seize power in Bavaria; they tried to lead the Reichswehr astray and march on Berlin. To usurp power, to incite the army to betray its oath, to try to unleash civil war, to expose the country to foreign reprisals—these are indeed the worst crimes that a citizen can commit against the laws and interests of his country. . . .

. . . [Ludendorff's] acquital signifies only that a German jury, forgetting Ludendorff's great military and political sins, forgetting his downfall in September 1918, and wanting only to remember the victory bulletins he once signed, did not dare to apply the law to him. This way of interpreting today's verdict undoubtedly may be unpleasant, but we should prefer the truth over the pleasant. And the truth is that Ludendorff has been acquitted for the reason he himself has underscored: because he is the highest personification of the party that preaches military revenge.

Le Temps, *April 2, 1924*

Imprisonment at Landsberg. L-R: Adolf Hitler, Emil Maurice, Hermann Kriebel, Rudolf Hess, and Friedrich Weber (1924).

party members. In a long, impassioned speech, using his reper-
tory of oratorical tricks, Hitler pounded away at the theme
that party workers must resume the political battle that had
been interrupted. The crowd of 4,000—sometimes hysterical,
often weeping—responded with all the emotional fervor Hitler
had expected. It took only two hours for him to regain the entire
movement. He was not surprised. His speech had been "a tactic
based on the precise calculation of human weaknesses, the
results of which must lead almost mathematically to success,"
as he had once put it.

These problems solved, Hitler set about establishing the Nazi

52

party at the national level. He had to adjust to a changed country. The situation in Germany was far different than it had been two years earlier. The terrible inflation had been halted by measures introduced by the central bank, and a more relaxed atmosphere prevailed in international policy.

Restored confidence in the government was expressed by the December, 1924, elections to the Reichstag. The centrist factions were strengthened, while the extremist parties were in a crisis. General Ludendorff's foray into independent politics went awry. His group won only 14 seats in the new election, less than half the number he had previously held. The KPD, or Communist

---

### IN LANDSBERG PRISON

• On his thirty-fifth birthday, which fell shortly after the trial, the parcels and flowers [Hitler] received filled several rooms. He had a large correspondence in addition to his visitors, and as many newspapers and books as he wished. Hitler presided at the midday meal, claiming and receiving the respect due to him as leader of the Party. . . .

*Alan Bullock, 1962* [4c]

### MEIN KAMPF

• . . . the book contains, first, an outline of the future German state and of the means by which it can one day become "lord of the earth," as the author puts it on the very last page; and, second, a point of view, a conception of life, or, to use Hitler's favorite German word, a *Weltanschauung*. That this view of life would strike a normal mind of the twentieth cen-

tury as a grotesque hodgepodge concocted by a half-baked, uneducated neurotic goes without saying. What makes it important is that it was embraced so fanatically by so many millions of Germans and that if it led, as it did, to their ultimate ruin it also led to the ruin of so many millions of innocent, decent human beings and especially outside Germany.

*William L. Shirer, 1960* [24g]

• . . . the book contains very little autobiography, but is filled with page after page of turgid discussion of Hitler's ideas, written in a verbose style which is both difficult and dull to read.

*Alan Bullock, 1962* [4d]

• Hitler's royalties—his chief source of income from 1925 on—were considerable when averaged over those first seven years. But they were nothing compared to those received in 1933, the year he became Chancellor. In his first year of office

Party, also lost seats, dropping from 62 to 45.

The new atmosphere persuaded Hitler that he would have to adopt a different strategy if he was to attain power. He ruled out armed insurrection against government institutions, which automatically would involve army opposition. Instead, he felt he would have to take over the country by legal means, making use of constitutional tools at hand, such as elections and government appointments, No more rathskeller putschs without guaranteed power behind him.

In February, 1925, Friedrich Ebert, the President of Germany, died, and elections to choose his successor were called for

---

*Mein Kampf* sold a million copies, and Hitler's income from the royalties, which had been increased from 10 to 15 per cent after January 1, 1933, was over one million marks (some $300,000), making him the most prosperous author in Germany and for the first time a millionaire. Except for the Bible, no other book sold as well during the Nazi regime, when few family households felt secure without a copy on the table. It was almost obligatory —and certainly politic—to present a copy to a bride and groom at their wedding, and nearly every school child received one on graduation from whatever school. By 1940, the year after World War II broke out, six million copies of the Nazi bible had been sold in Germany.

*William L. Shirer, 1960* [24h]

Mercedes. Although I've never driven myself, I've always been passionately keen on cars. I liked this Mercedes particularly. At the window of my cell, in the fortress, I used to follow with my eyes the cars going by on the road to Kaufbeunen, and wonder whether the time would return when I would ride in a car again. I discovered mine by reading a prospectus. At once I realised that it would have to be this or none. Twenty-six thousand marks, it was a lot of money! I can say that, as to what gives the Mercedes-Benz its beauty nowadays, I can claim the fatherhood. During all these years I've made innumerable sketches with a view to improving the line.

*Hitler, February 3, 1942* [12t]

### LEAVING LANDSBERG

• The first thing I did on leaving the prison at Landsberg, on the 20th December 1924, was to buy my supercharged

• He lost the apolitical elements who returned to their lethargy. He lost the fainthearted and the hangers-on, who had been moved to activism only by the hope of speedy triumph. The result was fewer but better National Socialists than there had been at the high point of the movement's

March. The Nazi party presented General Ludendorff as a candidate. Hitler, however, had not yet been able to consolidate his power, and Ludendorff received a dismal 211,000 votes out of the 27 million that were cast. In the second round of the elections, the Nazis backed the candidate of the central-right wing: Field Marshal Paul von Hindenburg. And in April, at the age of 77, von Hindenburg became President of the Republic. Hitler's support wasn't needed to assure von Hindenburg's victory, but it did ostensibly align Hitler with the parties of order and respectability.

early growth in the first months of 1924. Hitler, however, had developed patience. He turned his attention towards preparing for the long haul. He built a more effective party machinery. He reorganized the shattered SA and the debilitated propaganda machine. He spread his version of the Putsch—and waited for the new crises that he was sure would come and lift him to power. Like the Biblical Egyptians he tightened his belt and endured his seven lean years.

*Harold J. Gordon, Jr., 1972* [31g]

## A PREFERENCE FOR THE SPOKEN WORD

• Hitler showed a marked preference for the spoken over the written word. 'The force which ever set in motion the great historical avalanches of religious and political movements is the magic power of the spoken word. The broad masses of a population are more amenable to the appeal of rhetoric than to any other force.' The employment of verbal violence, the repetition of such words as 'smash,' 'force,' 'ruthless,' 'hatred,' was deliberate. Hitler's gestures and the emotional character of his speaking, lashing himself up to a pitch of near-hysteria in which he would scream and spit out his resentment, had the same effect on an audience. Many descriptions have been given of the way in which he succeeded in communicating passion to his listeners, so that men groaned or hissed and women sobbed involuntarily, if only to relieve the tension, caught up in the spell of powerful emotions of hatred and exaltation, from which all restraint had been removed. . . .

. . . Propaganda was not confined to the spoken word. There were the posters, always in red, the revolutionary colour, chosen to provoke the Left; the swastika and the flag, with its black swastika in a white circle on a red background, a design to which Hitler devoted the utmost care; the salute, the uniform, and the hierarchy of ranks.

*Alan Bullock, 1962* [4e]

# 4

# BUILDING THE PARTY

Political demagogues such as Hitler function best in a chaotic situation. But Germany's economic ills seemed on the way to recovery. The country had cleared the hurdle of postwar crisis, bringing its production to a competitive level with Great Britain. The number of unemployed dropped to a half-million in 1928, and basic salaries increased 10 per cent between 1925 and 1928. The shunning of such radical doctrines as Nazism was reflected in the results of the elections of May, 1928. The Social Democrats won an overwhelming victory with 9 million votes. The Nazi party placed ninth with 810,000 votes. The time was easy. Incidents of the terrible war and its aftermath receded into memory. In the midst of an economic boom that seemed permanent, a euphoric gaiety enveloped most Germans.

For Hitler, this was an onerous, though not totally negative, period. He was forced to limit his public appearances; in most sections of Germany, he was not allowed to organize political rallies. This gave him time to organize his party on a solid basis. The party broadened its base, covering almost all of Germany and winning followers in Austria and Czechoslovakia's Sudetenland.

He had also recruited a new, dynamic, and skilled aide, Josef Goebbels. An undersized, lame journalist with a degree in philosophy, Goebbels was a master propagandist. His press campaigns helped subvert Austria, Czechoslovakia, and Poland even before the German legions rolled in. The censorship system he developed to control communications in the Third Reich had never been equalled.

These were relatively easy years for the driven Führer-to-be. For weeks, he would seclude himself at a villa he rented on the Obersalzberg above Berchtesgaden, a small Alpine village in southeastern Germany, near the Austrian border. Now that he was free of party chores, he asked his widowed stepsister, Angela, to stay with him. She brought her daughter, Geli Rau-

### HITLER DECRIES WEAKNESS AND PACIFISM

• Internationalism is weakness in the life of nations. What is there that is born of internationalism? Nothing. The real values of human culture were not born of internationalism, but they were created by the whole heritage and tradition of the people (*das Volkstum*). When peoples no longer possess creative power they become international. Wherever there is weakness in regard to spiritual matters in the life of nations, internationalism makes its appearance. It is no coincidence that a people, namely, the Jews, which does not have any real creative ability is the carrier of this internationalism. It is the people with the least creative power and talent. It dominates only in the field of crooked and speculative economy.

*Hitler, May 1, 1923* [22h]

• We are enemies of cowardly pacifism because we recognize that according to the laws of nature struggle is the father of all things. We are enemies of democracy because we recognize that an individual genius represents at all times the best in his people and that he should be the leader. Numbers can never direct the destiny of a people. Only genius can do this. We are the deadly enemies of internationalism because nature teaches us that the purity of race and the authority of the leader alone are able to lead a nation to victory.

*Hitler, February 5, 1928* [22i]

• The fundamental motif through all the centuries has been the principle that force and power are the determining factors. All development is struggle. Only force rules. Force is the first law. A struggle has already taken place between original man and his primeval world. Only through struggle have states and the world become great. If one should ask whether this struggle is gruesome, then the only answer could be: For the weak, yes, for humanity as a whole, no.

*Hitler, November 26, 1926* [22j]

bal. Hitler had never married, but rumors of his sexual pro-
clivities had spread with his fame. There was an alleged, but
never verified, incident with a Vienna prostitute. In Vienna, too,
the callow Adolf had fallen in love with a girl named Stephanie.
She was from a wealthy family and the awkward youth would
admire her as she rode through the promenades in a carriage.
A friend of this period complained, "Stephanie gained more and
more influence over my friend, although he never spoke a
word to her." Now, in the late 1920s, there was Geli.

The relaxed political leader and his niece were often seen
together on the roads around Berchtesgaden, riding in a big

**A PERIOD OF PROSPERITY**

• The vast bulk of Germans lived in
relative prosperity during 1924 to 1929.
They saw improvement and hoped for
more. Art, the cinema, the theater, the
sciences flourished. The liberal elements
of the nation spread their beliefs. It is a
fallacy to suppose that Fascism was Germany's inexorable destiny. To regard anything in politics as inevitable is a faltalism
which ignores the dynamic laws of society.
Man is not entirely free, but within broad
limits he can affect and alter his fate. As
in all countries in modern times a tug-of-
war went on in Germany between Right
and Left, between employers and labor,
between conservatives and progressives.
The outcome of this conflict was not pre-
ordained, and the elements of peace,
democracy, and decency might have won.

Part of the responsibility for their defeat and the consequent advent of Hitler
rests on the shoulders of the rest of

Europe. The German Republic succumbed
because the War-winners did not do
enough to save it. They operated against
one another, against European unity and
against Germany. With England, France,
Russia, and Italy, as well as the minor nations, working at cross-purposes, Germany was the first big casualty.

*Louis Fischer, 1941* [30c]

**HITLER'S RESIDENCES**

• In 1926, succumbing to the intoxi-
cation of speed, he bought a supercharged
Mercedes and in 1928, the "Haus Wachen-
feld" which he had been renting since
1925 and two years later rebuilt to form
his "Berghof" residence. This was in the
Obersalzberg which he had got to know
and love through Dietrich Eckart who had
meanwhile died and where the Bechsteins
also had a villa. In his Munich domicile,

58

expensive automobile. Hitler loved impressive cars, despite his general neglect or avoidance of luxury. For instance, he disliked servants and kept only a skeleton domestic staff of six. But he enjoyed riding in anything that had power and was open to the air. He also enjoyed his niece's company. They frequented expensive restaurants and the Munich Opera House.

Hitler persevered in building his party, seeking both money and influential recruits. Such large industrialists as the Krupps and Fritz Thyssen secretly financed him. Thyssen headed the German steel trust. Baron Kurt von Schröder, the Cologne banker, and Otto Wolf, an iron magnate from the same city, were

on the other hand, the signs of his increasing prosperity became only slowly apparent. Since the war he had been renting a small and shabby room from a widow in the Thierschstrasse, with its worn linoleum and sparse furniture very much in keeping with a workers' leader and acrid opponent of the "Weimar bosses" and it was not until the end of 1929 that Hitler, who was almost conservative in such matters, moved into a nine-room flat in the high-class Prinzregentenplatz, retaining it to the end without, incidentally, interfering with the other tenants in the house.

*Helmut Heiber, 1960* [13e]

## A RALLY IN NUREMBERG

• Here in 1927, Brownshirts marched from all parts of Germany—50,000 of them had meanwhile been recruited—to admire their idol dressed for the first time in similar garb: Hitler had hitherto held his parades in a kind of robber costume comprising squashed homburg, trenchcoat and knickerbockers. For in the preceding, relatively quiet period Hitler had succeeded in perfecting a ritual for these political mass orgies centered on his person and culminating in ecstatic emotion at his appearance.

There, tightly packed in a hall, a crowd would wait for the speaker Adolf Hitler. He would be late—half an hour, an hour, but not because he was delayed. During this time he would be sitting somewhere in a Party office or in a hotel receiving every few minutes by telephone a report from the hall, a mood report describing how the tense audience was being slowly warmed up with staccato marching songs, how they were singing, what sort of effect the skillfully arranged announcements were making, how the masses reacted to the entry of the standard-bearers, how everything was building up to the moment when HE would make his entry amid deafening acclamation.

*Helmut Heiber, 1960* [13f]

won over. Even rich Jews contributed, donations that they later would deeply regret. Nazi party headquarters were located on Munich's Briennerstrasse. There, the Führer received visitors in a studio that had an enormous portrait of Frederick the Great.

Economic crisis, the birth of the Great Depression, came suddenly in 1929, catching the industrial nations unawares. The most serious financial shocks were felt in New York, where, in October, the stock exchanges crashed. The reverberations were felt throughout the world, with disastrous results. Adolf Hitler, who capitalized on disaster, discerned some propitious elements in the situation.

### HITLER SPEAKS OF GERMANY'S RIGHTS

• If men wish to live, then they are forced to kill others. The entire struggle for survival is a conquest of the means of existence which in turn results in the elimination of others from these same sources of subsistence. As long as there are peoples on this earth, there will be nations against nations and they will be forced to protect their vital rights in the same way as the individual is forced to protect his rights. . . .

. . . One is either the hammer or the anvil. We confess that it is our purpose to prepare the German people again for the role of the hammer. For ten years we have preached, and our deepest concern is: How can we again achieve power? We admit freely and openly that, if our Movement is victorious, we will be concerned day and night with the question of how to produce the armed forces which are forbidden us by the peace treaty. We solemnly confess that we consider every-

one a scoundrel who does not try day and night to figure out a way to violate this treaty, for we have never recognized this treaty. . . .

. . . We confess further that we will dash anyone to pieces who should dare to hinder us in this undertaking. . . . Our rights will never be represented by others. Our rights will be protected only when the German Reich is again supported by the point of the German dagger.

*Hitler, March 15, 1929* [22k]

### A VIEW OF HITLER

• Hitler responds to the vibrations of the human heart with the delicacy of a seismograph, or perhaps of a wireless receiving set, enabling him, with a certainty with which no conscious gift could endow him, to act as a loudspeaker proclaiming

He had built well. Between 1926 and 1929, the Nazi party swelled from 30,000 to 120,000. Hitler had constantly referred to the Weimar Republic as the "republic of betrayal" and to its leaders as the "Jew-ridden traitors." In an atmosphere of resurgent social disorder and uncertainty, his stance attracted progressively broader segments of the population. He formed an alliance with the monarchic nationalists to launch a violent public campaign against a new reparations treaty. He derided the Social Democrat government and its foreign policy.

In early 1930, the German economic crisis turned unalterably political. A financial reform law proposed by the government

the most secret desires, the least admissible instincts, the sufferings and personal revolts of a whole nation. But his very principle is negative. He only knows what he wants to destroy; he pulls down the walls without any idea of what he will build in their place. He is anti-Semitic, anti-Bolshevik, anti-capitalist. He denounces enemies, but knows no friends. He is devoid of any creative principle.

I remember one of my first conversations with him. It was nearly our first quarrel.

'Power!' screamed Adolf. 'We must have power!'

'Before we gain it,' I replied firmly, 'let us decide what we propose to do with it. Our programme is too vague; we must construct something solid and enduring.'

Hitler, who even then could hardly bear contradiction, thumped the table and barked:

'Power first. Afterwards we can act as circumstances dictate.'

'Hate,' I sometimes said to him, 'must be born of love. One must be capable of loving to know what is hateful and so have the strength to destroy it.'

He hated without knowing love. He was drunk with an ambition that was utterly without moral restraint, and had the pride of Lucifer, who wished to cast down God from His immortal throne.

*Otto Strasser, 1940* [26a]

### THE DEPRESSION AND THE NSDAP

• A sense of total discouragement and meaninglessness pervaded everything. Among the most striking concomitants of the Great Depression was an unprecedented wave of suicides. . . . The combination of public misery and the unfeelingness displayed by a hard-pressed and sickly capitalism led to the sense that everything was doomed to go down to destruction very soon. And, as always, such eschatological moods were accompanied by wild hopes that sprang up like weeds, along with irrational longings for a complete alteration of the world. Charlatans,

was defeated in parliament. Hindenburg, at the prompting of General Kurt von Schleicher, named a new chancellor, Heinrich Brüning. But Brüning's economic program was also rejected by the Reichstag. Because a definite majority could not be formed in support of the new government's position, the Reichstag was dissolved and new elections were called.

The electoral campaign was marked by violence. Both the Nazis and the Communists had their bully boys out, and on the streets neither side was discussing doctrine. The Communists were the most radical in their demands for a new social, international, and anticapitalistic system controlled by the working

astrologers, clairvoyants, numerologists, and mediums flourished. These times of distress taught men, if not to pray, pseudoreligious feelings, and turned their eyes willy-nilly to those seemingly elect personalities who saw beyond mere human tasks and promised more than normality, order, and politics as usual—who offered, in fact, to restore to life its lost meaning.

With remarkable instinct, Hitler grasped these cravings and knew how to make himself the object of them. . . .

. . . Hitler surpassed all his rivals in knowing how to give the color of a political decision to the personal wishes and despairs of the masses, and to insinuate his own aims into those who held the most divergent views and expectations. When spokesmen of other parties encountered the populace, their own lack of faith became apparent despite their efforts to win the people. They, too, had no answers and could count only on the solidarity of the powerless in the face of disaster. Hitler, on the other hand, took an optimistic and aggressive tone. He showed confidence in the future and cultivated his animosities.

*Joachim C. Fest, 1973* [6g]

● Here, again, was an economic crisis that would prove grist for Adolf's mill. It affected every class in the population, the factory workers, journeyman mechanics, laborers, farmers, the white collar workers, the lower middle class merchants and manufacturers, the professional groups and retired *rentiers*. It proved to be even worse than the inflation period following the war. Half the population was actually on the verge of starvation, many literally going hungry; young people out of school were unable to get jobs or begin hopeful careers.

*Morris D. Waldman, 1962* [33d]

● It was the rural and urban "middle class," in the broad sense of the term, which started and carried out the breakthrough of the NSDAP. The "panic of the middle class," which set in with the outbreak of the economic crisis, was sharpened by the fact that the middle class felt threatened not only economically but, more important, socially as well. The violent reaction which drove many of its members toward the radical Right arose out of a subjective

classes. To the German public, the Nazi program seemed less rigid and formulated than did the Communist program. The political touch was there in the Nazi approach for the astute observer to see. The Nazis were trying to satisfy many sectors of the nation. Before the elections, Hitler had expelled from his party the most militant left-wing faction—that headed by Otto Strasser. This reassured many of the industrial leaders, who, though their sympathies were with many of the goals of the Nazi movement, were apprehensive of the term "nationalization," a favored party term that appealed to the lower middle class and unemployed.

**Trying to Follow an Expert**
—Hungerford in the Pittsburgh *Post-Gazette*

feeling of crisis in a time of social upheaval in an industrial, democratic age. The power of the old middle class continued to decline within an expanding population; its nervous irritability and susceptibility to radical slogans was the result of this prestige loss as well as of economic plight. Out of a general desire for security after the catastrophe of the inflation, this group, after having for so long maintained an apolitical isolation from democracy, reacted in a markedly political fashion to the new crisis. And that was why it turned to the "new" party. . . .

. . . National Socialism's dynamics and appeal—like Fascism's—did not lie in a socially closed interest movement of the middle classes—that is, a class movement —but, on the contrary, in its emphasis on being a unifying movement of the most varied and antagonistic groups. The fact that it was able to develop this cohesive force across heterogeneous interests, considerations, and feelings is connected with the lack of fervor that accompanied the founding of the Republic in a time of military collapse and fear of a Left revolution.

*Karl Dietrich Bracher, 1969* [3a]

The elections were held on September 14, 1930, and, in a reversal of previous contests, the resounding victories went to the extremist parties. From 12 seats in the Reichstag, the Nazis soared to 107, capturing 6.4 million votes. The Communists' share jumped from 54 to 77 seats. The centrists—the Catholics, Democrats, and People's Party—were the big losers, along with the nationalistic right wing. Still, the winners, the Social Democrats, were in a state of crisis.

At this time, Hitler sponsored a reorganized, powerful army that would be capable of expressing the most authentic aspirations of the German people. At the same time, he had his own

## NATIONAL SOCIALISM

- [National Socialism's] roots lie certainly in the racial ideas of the pan-Germans of Austria and Germany, in their rabid anti-Semitism, their hatred of the Habsburgs and of the very principle of the Austrian State, in the movement away from Rome and the first beginnings of the enthusiasm for the myth of the pagan Teutons. . . .

. . . The aim of National Socialism is the complete revolutionizing of the technique of government, and complete dominance over the country by the leaders of the movement. The two things are inseparably connected: the revolution cannot be carried out without an élite ruling with absolute power, and this élite can maintain itself in power only through a process of continual intensification of the process of revolutionary disintegration. . . .

. . . National Socialism is action pure and simple, dynamics *in vacuo*, revolution at a variable tempo, ready to be changed at any moment. One thing it is not—doctrine or philosophy.

*Hermann Rauschning, 1939* [23a]

## SALVATION WITHOUT PARTICIPATION

- In time of turmoil, people turn to the parties of despair which aver that they have the only solution and that it lies in new men, new methods, new institutions. This seems logical to those who are suffering from the failure of the old. Mounting difficulties thus proved to be wind in the sails of the Communist and Nazi extremists.

The Nazis had this advantage: the Communists summoned citizens to rise and fight on the barricades against ruling cliques and mighty groups of business magnates. They anticipated bloody civil war, sacrifices, death, and initial chaos and poverty. Hitler, on the other hand, announced blandly that he would perform the task for them. If they believed in him they would be saved. He promised salvation without participation, and cure by faith. He was wise enough to insist that he would attain power by "legal" means.

*Louis Fischer, 1941* [30d]

personal army, the black-uniformed SS, or Schutz-Staffeln (defense troops). The original members of the SS were comparatively conservative and arsitocratic, and thus were in immediate conflict with the khaki-clad, boorish Brown Shirts upon whom Hitler had depended during his early political years. The Black Shirts, clearly an elite corps in the Hitler establishment, were sworn to absolute obedience. Under the leadership of Heinrich Himmler, it was to be the instrument through which Hitler ruled over the party, the armed forces, and the German citizenry.

These were busy months for Hitler, who now was considered a top-ranking politician. His party chores did not prevent him

Hitler, surrounded by members of the Brown Shirts, at Nazi party headquarters in Munich (about 1930).

from pursuing his interest in his niece, Geli. He lodged her in one of the nine rooms of his apartment on Munich's fashionable Prinzregentstrasse. In that room, in September, 1931, she was found dead, shot in the chest with a pistol, an apparent suicide. Hitler was overwrought. The shock also paralyzed his capacity for work, at least temporarily. Another woman, however, Eva Braun, would soon become his mistress and remain faithful until his death.

In the final months of 1931, political tensions worsened. Throughout Germany, the economic crisis took an increasing toll of workers' jobs. By the end of the following year, more than

### THE 1930 ELECTIONS

• We know, however, that in this election democracy must be defeated with the weapons of democracy. That is why we are entering into this election with all the energy that we possess; that is why in the next few weeks we will fight on from one end of Germany to the other. . . .

. . . If this Movement should achieve victory, internationalism, democracy, and pacifism will vanish in Germany and then the German people will rise up.

*Hitler, July 18, 1930* [221]

• September 14, 1930, became one of the turning points in the history of the Weimar Republic. It signified the end of the reign of democratic parties, and announced the initial death throes of the re-public. By the time the election results became available, toward three o'clock in the morning, everything had changed. With a single step the Nazi party had advanced into the anteroom of power, and its leader, object of ridicule and idolatry, the "drummer" Adolf Hitler, had become one of the key figures on the political scene. The fate of the republic was sealed, the Nazi press exulted. Now mopping-up operations could begin. . . .

. . . On the whole, most observers recognized the historic importance of what had happened. With varying accents they attributed it to the deep crisis of the party system or saw it as the expression of a spreading lack of faith in the liberal and capitalist systems, coupled with a desire for a fundamental change in all conditions of life. "Most of those who have given their vote to the extremist parties are not at all radical; they have only lost faith in the old way." No less than a third of the people had rejected the existing system in principle without knowing or asking what would follow it. There was talk of the "bitterness vote."

*Joachim C. Fest, 1973* [6h]

six million persons would be unemployed. Add to this the millions of impoverished middle-class individuals and the hundreds of thousands of professional men struggling to survive, and the sum is a situation ideal for exploitation by Adolf Hitler.

The Communists, too, seized on the economic chaos to win new support. Between the forces of Hitlerism and Communism, the government found it difficult to function. It blundered in search of solutions. The Reichstag was reduced to shrieking matches among representatives of its many factions. The government of Chancellor Heinrich Brüning, a centrist leader, maneuvered desperately to get events under control. For months,

• Adolf became the most dramatic figure in Europe. The press all over the world printed interviews with him. His assurances of good-will and love of peace were widely quoted and by many accepted at face value.

*Morris D. Waldman, 1962* [33e]

### NAZI HEADQUARTERS

• Hitler's headquarters is in the Brienner Strasse, Munich, in the ex-'Barlow Palace'. . . . The Brienner Strasse is one of the smartest streets in Munich. Hitler paid 500,000 marks for the Barlow Palace and spent as much again on alterations. The swastika flag flying from the roof can be seen a long way off. There are sentries on the door who check papers of everyone entering; they give an impression of extremely strict martial discipline. All of them are fine large military figures, hardfaced, and one can well imagine them giving their lives for their movement.

*Richard Breiting, 1931* [5a]

### TWO UNHAPPY WOMEN

• His evenings and nights belonged to Geli Raubal who quickly sensed, indeed knew, that her uncle had another girl friend whom he did not wish her to meet. Geli was in love with Hitler and Hitler was flirting outrageously with Eva Braun. Though neither girl knew the other, both were aware of the circumstances, suffered accordingly and reacted each in her own way. When [Geli], driven to despair, committed suicide in September 1931, Eva Braun saw her chance and took it. Hitler was in a state of deep depression. By her love and devotion she was able by degrees to revive his flagging spirits and thus make him entirely her own.

*Werner Maser, 1971* [17g]

• He did not attend Geli's interment in Vienna, for he was neither mentally nor physically fit enough to do so. Withdrawing from his associates, he became a prey

he had been ruling by decree based on emergency laws passed by the Reichstag. But popular discontent mounted as social services were curtailed and taxes escalated wildly.

Hitler's following had expanded so much that word spread that he would be taken into the government. President Hindenburg, who previously would have nothing to do with Hitler—an "upstart," he called Hitler—decided to receive him. The Nazi leader tried to flatter the aged Hindenburg by extolling the virtues of the army and the importance of its welfare. But the old general was not impressed. He did not even ask his visitor to sit down.

to self-reproach, and from then on never touched meat or food prepared with animal fats. No one might enter Geli's room in his Munich flat at No. 16 Prinzregentenplatz save for himself and his housekeeper, Frau Winter. He commissioned a bust of Geli from the sculptor Josef Thorak and subsequently had it placed in the Reich Chancellery, Adolf Ziegler, whose political views had earned him Hitler's approbation, was commissioned to paint her portrait which later occupied a place of honour, permanently decked with flowers, in the Berghof drawing-room. He was even mindful of his dead mistress in his private will of 2 May 1938: 'To my sister Angela I entrust the appointments of the room in my Munich flat formerly occupied by my niece Geli Raubal.'

*Werner Maser, 1971* [17h]

● Hitler knew all my employees, and it was among them that he first made the acquaintance of Eva Braun [in the early 1930's]. . . . Neither I myself nor any of my employees noticed that he paid her any particular attention. But not so Eva; she told all her friends that Hitler was wildly in love with her, and that she would bring him up to scratch and marry him.

Hitler on the other hand had no inkling of what was going on in Eva's mind, and he certainly had not the slightest intention of entering into a binding relationship, either then or later, with her. To him, she was just an attractive little thing, in whom, in spite of her inconsequential and featherbrained outlook—or perhaps just because of it—he found the type of relaxation and repose he sought.

*Heinrich Hoffmann, 1955* [14d]

● His attitude to women is reflected in his view that a 'great man' should 'keep a girl' for the satisfaction of his sexual needs and treat her as he deems fit, without compassion or a sense of responsibility, as though she were a mere chattel possessing no rights. As Eva Braun so aptly put it: 'When he says he loves me, he only means it at that moment.'

*Werner Maser, 1971* [17l]

Stymied, yet confident because of his rising popular support, Hitler announced his candidacy for the presidency in the spring of 1932. He had been assured of the invaluable backing of the big Ruhr industrialists. The race was fierce, with Hitler raving heatedly against the Brüning government, the economic situation, and, of course, the Treaty of Versailles. Hindenburg won the election, but Hitler emerged with 37 per cent of the ballots cast, or 13 million votes. Now no one could question Hitler's position as a power on the political scene.

Chancellor Brüning resigned the following May and, in the Reichstag election that resulted, the Nazis won 230 seats (against

President Paul von Hindenburg rides with the man who will replace him as head of Germany, Adolf Hitler.

133 for the Social Democrats). Although they did not have a majority of seats in the Reichstag, the Nazis were the largest single party in Germany. Hitler demanded the chancellorship twice. Each time, Hindenburg said, "No." He offered Hitler a cabinet post, which Hitler rejected. He would have the chancellorship or nothing.

Hitler realized that the number of warring factions in the Reichstag made formation of a government impossible. The Social Democrats and the center were squared against the Communist and Nazi extremists. Hindenburg named as his new Chancellor Franz von Papen, who, while a diplomat serving in

**NOT FOR PUBLICATION**

• I do not need the bourgeoisie; the bourgeoisie needs me and my movement. I have brought the concept of National-Socialism into the world and I shall carry through its ideas brutally and, if necessary, by force. In this I feel myself the emissary of Fate, the standard bearer as I am sometimes called, and with my Movement I shall thump the drum until Germany wakes up. . . . The bourgeoisie rules by intrigue, but it can have no foothold in my movement because we accept no Jews or Jewish accomplices into our Party. The bourgeoisie shows what it is capable of by the intrigues which it instigates against the Reichwehr, attempting to place a barrier between me and the officer corps. . . .

. . . the basic principle of my Party's economic programme should be made perfectly clear and that is the principle of authority. I want authority; I want individuality; I want everyone to keep what he has earned subject to the principle that the good of the community takes priority over that of the individual. But the State should retain control; every owner should feel himself to be an agent of the State; it is his duty not to misuse his possessions to the detriment of the State or the interests of his fellow-countrymen.

. . . Naturally an end must be put to trade union policy in its present form. The trade union policy has ruined us. Between 1925 and 1928 the budget increased by 18 milliard marks as a result of the trade union policy on wages, social security, unemployment insurance etc. The two milliard annual reparations payments are nothing compared to this. If today we had no more reparations to pay, social democracy, in other words trade union policy, would immediately demand wage increases to absorb the two milliard saved. That is nonsense and it should not be. As you will realise, I cannot say that at a public meeting. Similarly I cannot express my views on private property at a popular meeting in the same way as I have done to you.

*Hitler, May 1931* [5b]

the United States, engaged in espionage and sabotage. General von Schleicher, now the army chief and a major political force, forced von Papen's resignation. But the army was backing Hitler and refused to support von Schleicher.

The right-wing party, fearful of the mounting Communist influence in the dishevelled Reichstag, decided the Nazis would be most capable of meeting the Communist threat. German industrialists and financiers agreed to take over the Nazi party's debts. Hindenburg, under pressure from all sides, and by now described as senile, offered Adolf Hitler the chancellorship. In an official ceremony on January 10, 1933, in the presence of

Admirers reach out to touch their beloved Führer. In the 1930s, many couples named newborn sons Adolf, after the man they had chosen to lead them in the Third Reich.

### THE NAZI CAMPAIGN IN 1932

• Every constituency down to the most remote village was canvassed. In the little Bavarian hamlet of Dietramszell, where the President spent his summer holidays, the Nazis brought in some of their best speakers to capture 228 votes against the Field-Marshal's 157—a typical piece of Nazi spite. The walls of the towns were plastered with screaming Nazi posters; films of Hitler and Goebbels were made and shown everywhere (an innovation in 1932); gramophone records were produced which could be sent through the post, two hundred thousand marks spent on propaganda in one week alone. But, true to Hit-

President Hindenburg, Hitler was invested with the powers attendant on the offices of Reich Chancellor. As he emerged from the palace, the crowds hailed him with a lengthy ovation. In the evening, there was a long torchlight parade through the streets of Berlin. In a gala celebration of songs, slogans, and swastikas, the revelry continued through the morning hours.

Initially, the Hindenburg-led conservatives viewed the formation of the Hitler-led government as a triumph for their cause. They had a stable government and believed they could easily control that "upstart" Hitler and so use Nazism as a tool to achieve their own ends. After only one month, the patrician con-

ler's belief in the superiority of the spoken word, the main Nazi effort went into organizing a chain of mass meetings at which the principal Nazi orators, Hitler, Goebbels, Gregor Strasser, worked their audiences up to hysterical enthusiasm by mob oratory of the most unrestrained kind.

*Alan Bullock, 1962* [4f]

## HITLER BECOMES CHANCELLOR

• Hitler was to play his old role of 'Drummer', the barker for a circus-show in which he was now to have a place as partner and his name at the top of the bill, but in which the real decisions would be taken by those who outnumbered him by eight to three in the Cabinet. This was *Realpolitik* as practised by Papen, a man who—as he prided himself—knew how to distinguish between the reality and the shows of power.

Rarely has disillusionment been so complete or so swift to follow. Those who, like Papen, believed they had seen through Hitler were to find they had badly under-

estimated both the leader and the movement. For Hitler's originality lay in his realization that effective revolutions, in modern conditions, are carried out with, and not against, the power of the State: the correct order of events was first to secure access to that power and then begin his revolution. Hitler never abandoned the cloak of legality; he recognized the enormous psychological value of having the law on his side. Instead he turned the law inside out and made illegality legal.

*Alan Bullock, 1962* [4g]

## THE REICHSTAG FIRE

• Together with Hitler, I had accepted an invitation to dine with Goebbels . . . on the 26th February, 1933. . . .

. . . The telephone bell interrupted the somewhat frivolous conversation. Goebbels himself answered it, and I remember the conversation as well as if it had occurred yesterday.

servatives discovered this was an illusion.

Hitler's first act as Chancellor was to dissolve the Reichstag and call for new elections. The trusting Hindenburg expressed delight that the new government was seeking the support of the people. He forgot that Hitler now had the powerful instruments of government at his fingertips. Goebbels took over direct control of the radio and press. Goering was installed as Minister for Internal Affairs in Prussia. For funds, the national treasury was at their command.

Goebbels outdid himself in the stream of propaganda that engulfed the nation. The bully boys were out cracking heads

'Goebbels here—who's that? Oh—hullo, Hanfstängl! What is it? . . . What!? I can't believe it! Half a minute—I'll hand you over to the Führer himself!'

'Hullo, Hanfstängl, what's up? . . . Oh, get along with you!' (Hitler seemed to be highly amused.) 'Are you seeing things—or have you had a drop too much whiskey? What? You can see the flames from your room?'

Hitler turned to us, 'Hanfstängl says the Reichstag building is on fire. . . .'

We looked out of the window, and the sky over the Tiergarten was in fact blood-red.

'It's the Communists!' suddenly shouted Hitler in furious voice. . . . 'We'll have a showdown over this! I must go at once! Now I've got them!'

*Heinrich Hoffmann, 1955* [14a]

● During the Reichstag fire, I went in the middle of the night to the offices of the *Völkischer Beobachter*. It took half an hour before I could find anyone to let me in . . . eventually some sub-editor appeared heavy with sleep. He was quite in-

capable of grasping what I was telling him and kept on repeating: "But really! there's no one here at this time of night; I must ask you to come back during business hours!" "Are you mad!" I cried. "Don't you realise that an event of incalculable importance is actually now taking place!" In the end I got hold of Göbbels, and we worked till dawn preparing the next day's edition.

*Hitler, August 21, 1942* [12e]

● That night there was an official dinner at the French Embassy. The Reich Minister of Finance, Schwerin von Krosigck, was present. Halfway through the meal, at about nine, the embassy porter passed me a note which read: "The Reichstag is on fire." I immediately excused myself and moved to one of the windows overlooking the garden; from there I could see the dome of the Reichstag. Its glass cupola blazed as scarlet as though fireworks were being set off below. I returned to the dining room to inform my guests of what was happening. Their reception of this news betrayed their stupefaction. But Krosigck, who was not a Nazi—at least not at the

to create turmoil and an atmosphere of fear. Ernst Röhm, who was fighting a war as a mercenary in Bolivia, was recalled to direct the strong-arm squads. The objective was simple: one German party with all others subjected to continued intimidation and terror. If Hindenburg and other members of the German electorate were surprised at the Nazi version of an election campaign, they could have read all about it in *Mein Kampf*.

The violence culminated on February 27, 1933, with the burning of the Reichstag. Both symbolically and practically, the destruction of the German parliament was the perfect scenario to signal the end of national freedom. Nazi propagandists im-

Hitler reads the newspaper while relaxing on the veranda of his mountain home above Berchtesgaden, in southeastern Germany.

Germans watch the burning of the Reichstag on February 28, 1933. Hitler insisted that the Communists were responsible for the fire.

mediately assailed the Communists as the arsonists, accusing them of plotting a coup to take over the country. The Nazis claimed they had documentary proof of Communist involvement. The next day Hitler proclaimed a state of emergency, which, in effect, cancelled all guarantees of personal and social liberties. Goering, as head of the Prussian state police, swore in thousands of Brown Shirts as special constables to roust the Reds from their homes and meeting places. A mentally retarded Dutch Communist, Marinus van der Lubbe, later was convicted and executed for setting the fire. Did he set it? Who—if anyone—was behind him? Such puzzles remain unsolved.

time—could not disguise his joy. *"Gott sei dank!"* he exclaimed "Thank God!" . . .

. . . For the most part my fellow diplomats and the French and Anglo-Saxon press correspondents stoutly denied the official version and believed a Nazi plot more likely. . . .

. . . Today nobody, save in Germany, can possibly doubt that the Reichstag fire was set by a dozen Brown militiamen, who entered and left the building through the secret corridor linking it to the residence of Goering, the Reichstag President. The trial held in late 1933 at Leipzig failed to reveal this, but it did at least establish the innocence of Torgler [a Communist deputy] and of the Bulgarians indicted. It also proved that the luckless Van der Lubbe, so prone to acknowledge his guilt, was a moron, a human wreck, and had probably been drugged in order, as decoy, to divert suspicion from the true criminals. The press announced that he had been sentenced to death and executed, but rumors in Berlin asserted that his family, claiming his body, had never been able to obtain possession.

*André François-Poncet, 1946* [7a]

• At a luncheon on the birthday of the Fuehrer in 1942 the conversation turned to the topic of the Reichstag building and its artistic value. I heard with my own ears when Goering interrupted the conversation and shouted: "The only one who really knows about the Reichstag is I, because I set it on fire"

*General Franz Halder, at the Nuremberg trial* [21a]

[Goering, at Nuremberg, denied that he had had any part in the Reichstag fire.]

• The whole truth about the Reichstag fire will probably never be known. Nearly all those who knew it are now dead, most of them slain by Hitler in the months that followed. Even at Nuremberg the mystery could not be entirely unraveled, though there is enough evidence to establish beyond a reasonable doubt that it was the Nazis who planned the arson and carried it out for their own political ends. . . .

*William L. Shirer, 1960* [24i]

# 5
## THE NAZI TAKEOVER AND THE TERROR

Despite its campaign of unparalleled terror and violence, the Nazi party was unable to win an absolute majority in the elections of March 5. The tally was 288 seats out of 647, or 43.9 per cent. The Social Democrats won 7 million votes and 120 seats. The Communists collected 4.8 million votes and 81 seats.

This was to be the last formal election in Nazi Germany that, in any sense, could be called proper. If Hitler could not dominate the will of the people through the ballot box, he would dominate them through government. He issued a decree that vested the government with dictatorial powers. He ordered all Communist members of the Reichstag and a dozen Social Democrats arrested. Less than three weeks after the Reichstag election, the Hitler forces, assisted by the Catholics, rammed a so-called constitutional delegation law—the Enabling Act—through parliament. This law gave the Führer legislative power for four years. Sponsors of the bill were the SA and the Goering-run police force. Storm troopers with pistols lined the aisles of the Reichstag meeting, which was held in temporary quarters in an opera house. Hitler addressed the legislators, crying, "Choose between peace and war!" Outside in the square, storm troopers roared in menacing cadence, "The law or death!" German democracy had ended.

President Hindenburg declared that the Nazi swastika, Hitler's party emblem, be incorporated in the black and white ensign as part of the official flag of Germany.

Hitler now proceeded ruthlessly to destroy any possible source of opposition, backed by his tens of thousands of storm troopers and SS men who blanketed German cities and towns like an army of occupation. He abolished the Socialist, Communist, and Democratic parties. He began a systematic drive to fill all government and civil-service positions with Nazi party members. All elements considered dangerous to the regime—Jews, Marxists, and Democrats—were tossed out of their jobs. Offices of

## IN POWER

• . . . The National Socialism that came to power in 1933 was no longer a nationalist but a revolutionary movement. The failure of the middle class to realize this was a fatal error. It was no longer possible to rid the movement of its revolutionary character; from its very nature it grew irresistibly in extremism. This was not apparent even to the members of the party. Even party members were startled when, in the spring of 1933, the practical steps taken by their leaders began to reveal the realities behind all the patriotic oratory— the unashamed pursuit of power and of key positions, and the cynical resort to a brutality hitherto inconceivable.

This apparent change in the character of National Socialism (in reality it was no change but simply a revelation of the true character of the movement) was so striking that the suspicion arose among members of the party that it was the work of enemies within the party who were out to compromise the movement.

*Hermann Rauschning, 1939* [23b]

• The aim of this great uprising is the inner and actual victory over November 1918: . . . the end of the German Revolution must come only with the end of the November criminals, the end of their system, the end of their existence. We will track down these men into their last lurking-places, we will not pause or rest until the last trace of this poison is removed from the body of our people.

*Hitler, May 7, 1933* [1a]

• Nothing can prove that more clearly than the mere conception of a class-war— the slogan that the rule of the *bourgeoisie* must be replaced by the rule of the proletariat. That means that the whole question becomes one of a change in a class-dictatorship, while our aim is the dictatorship of the people, i.e. the dictatorship of the whole people, the community. We do not regard position or standing in life as decisive; all such considerations fade into insignificance before Destiny, before the millennia.

*Hitler, May 10, 1933* [1b]

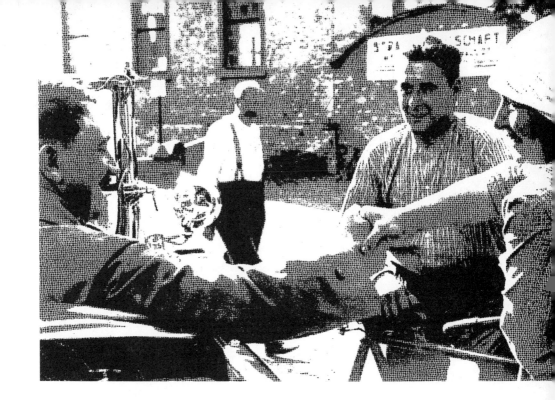

Hitler greets a peasant woman in Oldenburg. Photos such as this were distributed to show Hitler's "intimate, human side, of which little had been heard" prior to his appointment as Chancellor.

The swastika—"a symbol it really is!" wrote Hitler in *Mein Kampf.* "In red we see the social idea of the movement, in white the nationalist idea, in the swastika the mission of the struggle for the victory of the Aryan man."

opposition newspapers were wrecked. Within three months, all political parties other than the Nazi party had been disbanded or, like the Catholic Centrists, had voluntarily disbanded themselves.

In May, a new law terminated the system of direct bargaining between management and labor. Work contracts henceforth were to be stipulated by the government. In smashing the trade unions, Hitler crushed the last important element of opposition to his regime.

The thoroughness of the Nazi takeover was awe-inspiring. Even the Reich's federal system was undermined with the crea-

• To say that most German statesmen and politicians outside the Government's charmed circle were scared to death last week, would be understatement. Panic made cowards of the bravest of brave German Socialists and Communists. Even Catholics trembled. . . . It was accurately said that in less than two weeks Chancellor Hitler has reduced his opponents to a lower level of groveling fear than did Premier Mussolini in the two years after the March on Rome. . . .

. . . With Jews still being beaten and Jewish stores raided or closed throughout the Reich last week, non-Jews gradually recovered a feeling that any further Nazi violence would almost certainly not be directed against them, unless they happened to be Marxists.

"We are going to extirpate Marxism!" shouted Captain Göring amid applause from the conservative Pomeranian Landbund. "I am going to keep my fist on the neck of these creatures until they are finished. We are not only going to extirpate the pest but we are going to tear the word Marxism out of every book. In 50 years nobody in Germany is going to know what the word means."

Time, *March 27, 1933, p. 15, 16*

• [Germany] celebrated Hitler's forty-fourth birthday with a flourish. There were mass meetings, parades, gala performances at opera houses, patriotic plays at State theaters, and special services in churches. The day was declared a holiday. . . .

Because Hitler had said that edelweiss, a white Alpine bloom, was his favorite flower, thousands of Storm Troopers and school children sold artificial edelweiss on street corners. Money collected in this way was applied to a fund for enfeebled children.

Newsweek, *April 29, 1933, p. 13*

tion of new federal officers called governors, who replaced local office holders.

The Nazi party was Adolf Hitler. And Germany was to become Adolf Hitler. The party certainly was not socialist, though it advocated, in the name of the greater good, appropriation by the state of whatever it wanted. It was, indeed, nationalist and muzzily preached about Germany's rightful place among the nations. But over and above all else, it was authoritarian, totalitarian, and entirely wrapped into the peculiarly compelling personality of Adolf Hitler.

Though Hitler and his henchmen were muzzy in talking about

## THE ATTRACTION OF FORCE

• This breakdown of law and order, of the ordinary security of everyday life, not from any weakness or collapse of authority, but with the connivance of the State, was a profound shock to the stability of a society already shaken by the years of depression and mass unemployment. Yet violence, if it repelled, also attracted many, especially among the younger generation. It was indeed a characteristic part of revolutionary idealism. For 1933, like other revolutionary years, produced great hopes, a sense of new possibilities, the end of frustration, the beginning of action, a feeling of exhilaration and anticipation after years of hopelessness. Hitler recognized this mood when he told the German people to hold up their heads and rediscover their old pride and self-confidence. Germany, united and strong, would end the crippling divisions which had held her back, and recover the place that was her due in the world. Many people believed this in 1933 and thought that a new era had begun. Hitler succeeded in releasing pent-up energies in the nation, and in re-creating a belief in the future of the German people. It is wrong to lay stress only on the element of coercion, and to ignore the degree to which Hitler commanded a genuine popular support in Germany—so much less, as Mill once remarked, do the majority of the people prefer liberty to power. The law introducing the plebiscite [Law of July 14, 1933] is evidence of the confidence Hitler felt that he could carry a majority of the German people with him, once he had come to power and broken all organized resistance. To suppose that the huge votes which he secured in these plebiscites were soley, or even principally, due to the Gestapo and the concentration camps is to miss what Hitler knew so well, the immense attraction to the masses of force plus success.

*Alan Bullock, 1962* [4h]

## EFFICIENCY AND DISCIPLINE

• Hitler grasped what other parties (to their honor) failed to see: "that the

Germany, they were horrifyingly clear in holding up the German, the Nordic, the Aryan, as the superman whose destiny it was to rule the "undermen." The undermen were those people of Slavic origin. But the great threat to Germany and German racial purity were the Jews. Hitler always was quite clear about the Jews.

Wholesale arrests were taking place in Germany. Members of groups that might oppose the government in any way were carted off to newly opened concentration camps, where political prisoners often were beaten and half-starved. Christians were allowed to practice their religion as long as they did not attempt

strength of a political party is by no means proportionate to the greatness and independence of the intelligence of the individual members, but rather to the disciplined obedience with which its members follow the spiritual leadership." Victory falls to "whoever has the most efficient leadership and at the same time the most disciplined, blindly obedient, best-drilled troop. . . . A company of two hundred men of equal intellectual ability would in the long run be harder to discipline than one consisting of a hundred and ninety of inferior intellectual ability and of ten more highly educated."

*Konrad Heiden, 1936* [10h]

### INDIVIDUAL LIBERTY

• A very large measure of individual liberty is not necessarily the sign of a high degree of civilisation. On the contrary, it is the limitation of this liberty, within the framework of an organisation which incorporates men of the same race, which is

the real pointer to the degree of civilisation attained.

If men were given complete liberty of action, they would immediately behave like apes. No one of them could bear his neighbour to earn more than he did himself, and the more they lived as a community, the sharper their animosities would become. Slacken the reins of authority, give more liberty to the individual, and you are driving the people along the road to decadence.

*Hitler, April 11, 1942* [12g]

### THOUGHTS ON THE CHURCH

• . . . Hitler has a deep respect for the Catholic church and the Jesuit order; not because of their Christian doctrine, but because of the "machinery" they have elaborated and controlled, their hierarchical system, their extremely clever tactics, their knowledge of human nature, and their wise use of human weaknesses in ruling over believers. Hitler wants to see the points of

to apply its moral precepts to Nazi Germany. If they did, there were the concentration camps. The media, the arts, anyone who threatened opposition, faced the terror of the Gestapo and the camps.

The Jews, however, didn't have to threaten opposition—they went to the camps anyway; they faced terror and beatings no matter what they did. While Jews constituted less than one per cent of the German population, the Nazis aroused the latent bigotry of the Germans by claiming that the Jews held disproportionate power in Germany and were responsible for the country's ills. The hated Communists, said the Nazis, were part

the National Socialist program regarded as analogous to the Church's venerable *Credo,* the confession of faith. He is aware that for fifteen hundred years the Church has withstood all assaults from logical criticism on its ancient creed. He sees that anything can be done with a creed of that sort, no matter how irrational or inconsistent. The flock of believers will accept anything, and will listen to no reasoned opposition.

*Hermann Rauschning, 1939* [23c]

• It's a real scandal that we must give the German Churches such extraordinarily high subsidies. It isn't like that anywhere else, even in the most fundamentally Catholic countries, with the exception of Spain. Unless I'm mistaken, our Churches are still at present receiving nine hundred million marks a year. Now, the priests' chief activity consists in undermining National-Socialist policy. The habit of exploiting the State goes back a long way. . . .

. . . After this war [World War II], I'll take the necessary steps to make the re-

cruiting of priests extraordinarily difficult. In particular, I'll no longer allow children, from the age of ten and upwards, to devote their lives to the Church, when they've absolutely no notion what they're undertaking—in accepting celibacy, for example.

*Hitler, April 7, 1942* [12h]

• The heaviest blow that ever struck humanity was the coming of Christianity. Bolshevism is Christianity's illegitimate child. Both are inventions of the Jew. The deliberate lie in the matter of religion was introduced into the world by Christianity. Bolshevism practises a lie of the same nature, when it claims to bring liberty to men, whereas in reality it seeks only to enslave them. In the ancient world, the relations between men and gods were founded on an instinctive respect. It was a world enlightened by the idea of tolerance. Christianity was the first creed in the world to exterminate its adversaries in the name of love. Its key-note is intolerance.

*Hitler, July 11, 1941* [12l]

Storm Troopers drag a Jewish prisoner through town in a junk wagon.

Hitler greets his comrades in Nuremberg's City Hall (Nazi Reich's Party Day—August 30, 1933).

of an international Jewish conspiracy—an alleged conspiracy that, by the way, also included wealthy financiers.

On April 1, 1933, Hitler ordered a nationwide boycott of Jews. Jewish-looking persons were beaten in the streets. The original intent was to get rid of Germany's Jews—Hitler had not yet hit on his "final solution" for European Jewry. He wanted, at this point, to make Germany "Jew-free." In 1933, Jews were excluded from a number of fields, including public office, civil service, all forms of media, and even farming. In 1934, they were banned from the stock exchanges.

On September 15, 1935, the Nuremberg Laws deprived Jews

## THE NORDIC RACE

• The borderline between man and the animal is established by man himself. The position which man enjoys today is his own accomplishment. We see before us the Aryan race which is manifestly the bearer of all culture, the true representative of all humanity. All inventions in the field of transportation must be credited to the members of a particular race. Our entire industrial science is without exception the work of the Nordics. All great composers from Beethoven to Richard Wagner are Aryans, even though they were born in Italy or France. Do not say that art is international. The tango, the shimmy, and the jazzband are international but they are not art. Man owes everything that is of any importance to the principle of struggle and to one race which has carried itself forward successfully. Take away the Nordic Germans and nothing remains but the dance of apes.

*Hitler, April 2, 1927* [22m]

## ATTACKING THE JEWS

• The elimination of Jews from German public life (if not from Germany altogether) was one of the chief promises of National-Socialist propagandists and apparently rarely failed to elicit approval. Gregor Strasser promised (October 31, 1931) that the National-Socialists would put an end to Jewry in Germany. Pastor Peperkorn told the Prussian Diet that the Jews must get out. Deputy Kube announced to the same august body (June 2, 1932) that "when we clean house, the Exodus of the Children of Israel will be a child's game in comparison." The so called Boxheimer documents seized by the police on National-Socialists announced the preparation of obligatory service for all but Jews, and food only for those who served. Clearly, the Jews were to starve.

A Jewish organization published a long list of attacks on isolated Jews. In Pustutten, men of the Third Empire set dogs on a Jewish merchant. Smearing Jewish walls with taunts, obscenities and swastika sym-

of German citizenship and forbade marital or extramarital relations between Jews and Aryans. In the next few years, additional decrees made life—indeed, subsistence—barely possible
for a Jew in Germany. Even if a Jewish family had money, they
often encountered signs in food shops that declared, "Jews Not
Admitted." By the end of 1938, the Jews were forbidden to practice law or medicine or engage in business.

Crystal Night, the night of November 9, 1938, and the week
that followed it—the "week of broken glass"—put the final seal
of doom on those Jews who remained in Germany, and eventually on those who remained in the German-occupied countries.

SA members with posters that read:
"Germans, defend yourselves. Do not
buy from Jews."

Crystal Night aftermath:
A Jew cleans up glass from his
broken shop windows.

The Nazi pretext for a carefully organized campaign of "spontaneous" murder and pillage was the shooting of a minor German embassy official in Paris by a 17-year-old Jewish refugee, Herschel Grunszpan. Throughout Germany, Jewish homes and stores were wrecked, synagogues desecrated and burned, and many thousands of Jews either killed, injured, or arrested. For their part as victims, the Jews were fined $400 million. It was the precursor to what would come later—death camps, diabolical medical experiments, the panoply of incredible cruelty, and the death of some six million people.

Hitler's fanatical anti-Semitism was undoubtedly sincere, but

bols had become the pastime of thousands of children. In many schools Jewish children were enduring hell at the hands of their merciless Christian companions. Many a small merchant was hounded from the small town where his family had lived for generations, by unceasing boycott and persecution. At one moment the Nationalist students at the University of Berlin coolly demanded the dismissal of all Hebrew students.

And the courts? Surely all decent Germans protested against such villainy and severely punished the offenders?

They did not.

*Edgar Ansel Mowrer, 1939* [20a]

• [On April 1, 1933] SA columns covered the capital, arresting or beating such Jews as they encountered. They broke into the most frequented cafés and restaurants of the Kurfürstendamm, and, wielding their blackjacks, expelled all Jewish clients. Militiamen were detailed to stand outside shops and prevent anyone from entering. Inside, the shopkeepers were soundly drubbed, their stock rifled and money extorted from them under threats of future brutality. These operations continued all day long at the tune of *"Juda verrecke, let Jewry perish!"*

*André François-Poncet, 1946* [7b]

• . . . prankish Storm Troopers rounded up hundreds of Jews in Vienna's parks, marshaled them into parade formation, roared with laughter when they forced them to perform a burlesque of the goose step through the city's amusement centre. The troopers made Jewish cafe patrons scrub floors and wash windows, and escorted through the streets customers from Jewish stores who were forced to carry signs reading: "I am an Aryan pig, I bought from a Jewish shop". . . .

. . . In Manhattan arrived Führer Fritz Kuhn of the German-American Bund after a trip to Germany and Austria. Met by two gray-coated, black-trousered Bund officers, Führer Kuhn brought back a message from German Jews to American Jews. "I've talked with lots and lots of

in the early mid-1930s, it also served a purpose. Because, while much had changed in Germany, it was useful to take the people's minds off what was not changed.

What remained unchanged was the German economy. Millions of people were still unemployed. The government froze wages and appointed a General Economic Council, composed of industrialists such as Thyssen and Krupp, to advise on business solutions. Nationalization of key industries was to follow. To reduce unemployment, vast building and public works projects were launched. Foreign workers were excluded from jobs. In addition, Hitler advocated repudiation of reparations, aboli-

Jews in Germany," Kuhn said, "and they all told me this: 'Tell the Jews in America to let us alone. We're all right.' Thousands of Jews are returning to Germany and I was really surprised to see how many Jewish stores were open."

Time, *May 9, 1938, p. 16–17*

And the accused, in a fit of anger, cried out:

"It's not a crime to be a Jew. I am not a dog. I have the right to live; the Jewish people have a right to the earth, too. Everywhere I have appeared, I have been tracked down like a beast."

Le Figaro, *November 9, 1938, p.7*

### CRYSTAL NIGHT

• . . . the accused [Herschel Grunszpan] repeated that his parents had lived in Germany for twenty-eight years. Twenty thousand persons such as he, after having seen their laboriously acquired property sold, have been pursued without being able to carry even their clothes.

"Before leaving Hanover," he said, "I wrote to President Roosevelt. I asked him to intervene, to permit us to go to America, where I would have worked to feed my relations."

Grunszpan then explained that he had studied Judaism at Yeshiva (rabbinical seminary), to learn why he was a Jew.

• BERLIN, November 10—A kind of madness has seized the German people, and today their hatred of Jews reached a peak. Jews of all ages, both men and women, have been hunted down, even in their homes. Only two have been killed, but in Vienna such a wave of terror has seized the Jews that twenty people have committed suicide.

In Berlin, a vicious crowd has been rampaging through the city since morning, destroying all the shop windows of Jewish stores, pillaging, stealing, and burning— with fury and with joy—everything it finds in its path. Few policemen were in the streets; those that were visible looked on indifferently at the terrible pillage.

tion of unearned income, and reduction of interest rates.

Under the ashes of law and order, beneath the official avowals of confidence, there was discontent—and apathy. In factories, schools, and social organizations, Germans felt helpless. They watched, at first incredulous and then with a feeling of impotence, the destruction of all their mass organizations—political parties, unions, and newspapers.

The reign of terror was forcing many teachers and intellectuals to flee their homeland. A few remained at the universities and other cultural institutions to carry on an underground movement. They and some other Germans developed a deep

Any arrests that were made were of Jews, who were trying to protect their property. . . .

All the important synagogues, in Berlin as well as in Hamburg and cities of lesser importance, either have been set on fire or have been completely emptied of any precious objects they contained. Foreigners who tried to take photographs of the burning synagogues were escorted to the police station, where their cameras were confiscated.

Le Figaro, *November 11, 1938*

we can only be astonished at this reaction. For how thankful they must be that we are releasing apostles of culture and placing them at the disposal of the rest of the world. In accordance with their own declarations they cannot find a single reason to excuse themselves for refusing to receive this most valuable race in their own countries. Nor can I see a reason why the members of this race should be imposed upon the German nation, while in the states which are so enthusiastic about these "splendid people," their settlement should suddenly be refused with every imaginable excuse.

Hitler, *January 30, 1939* [22n]

## EXPULSION FROM GERMANY

• German culture, as its name alone shows, is German and not Jewish, and therefore its management and care will be entrusted to members of our own nation. If the rest of the world cries out with a hypocritical mien against this barbaric expulsion from Germany of such an irreplaceable and culturally valuable element,

## BURNING BOOKS

• On May 10, bonfires fed by "un-German" books will blaze at scores of German universities. Between now and then, students will weed out their bookshelves

Berlin: Young Nazis salute their leader
during a book-burning (May 19, 1933).

dissatisfaction with their regime, but it was vague, disorganized, and rarely took the form of action. Even among the Nazis themselves, some were aghast at the extremism of Hilter's totalitarian policies.

The Nazi movement presented a monolithic front to outsiders. But as often happens when diverse interests join in mutual discontent, success brought with it factionalism. For the radical and violent wing of the party, the annihilation of Marxists had represented only the first phase of a revolution. Now, they felt that the Nazis should deal similarly with the conservative establishment that controlled the nation—the big industrialists and Prus-

and the bookshelves of their classmates. The German Student Corporation, an organization of students recognized by the Hitler Government, has so decreed.

"Our most dangerous antagonists are the Jews and their satellites," reads a statement of the organization's principles. "The Jew can speak only Jewish. When he writes in German he lies . . . We therefore demand . . . that Jewish writings appear in Hebrew . . . of the German students we demand . . . the will and the ability to overcome Jewish intellectualism and the phenomena of liberal degeneration associated therewith."

Newsweek, *April 22, 1933, p. 12*

● One of Goebbels' actions which was by no means unanimously approved and which called forth the sharpest possible criticism in Party circles was the famous book-bonfire in the Berlin Gendarmemarkt.

I did not hesitate to tell Hitler quite frankly what I thought of it. 'Things like that,' I said, 'merely bring the Reich and the Party into disrepute, especially when they are carried out wholesale—and all they accomplish is to raise a few cheap cheers from the mob and rabble. Lots of the stuff burnt was certainly rubbish; but lots of it consisted of works of established international reputation. Why—even dictionaries were burnt, simply because they had been compiled by Jews!'

*Heinrich Hoffmann, 1955* [14b]

## THE MEDIOCRITY OF NUMBERS

● In all ages it was not democracy that created values, it was individuals. However, it was always democracy that ruined and destroyed individuality. . . .

Nations have always gone to ruin on the principle of democracy. If Germany has declined in the last fourteen years, it is because the advocacy of the principle of democracy had gone so far that its patrons and representatives in Germany were actually subject to the mediocrity of numbers, whose very sovereignty they preached. They themselves had become so inferior,

Sketches of Nazi enemies—"saboteurs of the Führer's work"—decorate this SA truck.

so puny and dwarfish, that they did not even possess the right to lift themselves above the masses. There has never yet been a regime or a government which gave up the ghost in a more dismal, more lamentable, and more inferior manner than the representatives of the recent system.

*Hitler, March 2, 1933* [22o]

● In that we deny the principle of parliamentary democracy we strike the strongest blow for the right of the nation to the self-determination of its own life. For in the parliamentary system we see no genuine expression of the nation's will—a will which cannot logically be anything else than a will to the maintenance of the nation—but we do see a distortion, if not a perversion, of that will. The will of a nation to the self-determination of its being manifests itself most clearly and is of most use when its most capable minds are brought forth. They form the representative leaders of a nation, they alone can be the pride of a nation—certainly never the parliamentary politician who is the product of the ballot box and thinks only in terms of votes.

*Hitler, September 1, 1933* [22p]

## A LETTER TO RÖHM

● My dear Chief of Staff,

The fight of the National Socialist Movement and the National Socialist Revolution were rendered possible for me by the consistent suppression of the Red Terror by the SA. If the army has to guarantee the protection of the nation against the world beyond our frontiers, the task of the SA is to secure the victory of the National Socialist Revolution and the existence of the National Socialist State and the community of our people in the domestic sphere. When I summoned you to your present position, my dear Chief of Staff, the SA was passing through a serious crisis. It is primarily due to your services if after a few years this political instrument could develop that force which

sian aristocrats, their reactionary representatives in politics and among the army officers.

There also was discontent among those members of the conservative establishment who had cast their lot with Hitler. Cabinet members who had expected to control Hitler found themselves instead acting as mere executors of the Führer's orders. Proud army officers found themselves competing against Röhm and his SA, a super-street gang of two-million armed men.

These conflicts exploded in the spring of 1934, when a new problem arose. Hindenburg's deteriorating health signalled the imminent designation of a new President of the Reich.

---

enabled me to face the final struggle for power and to succeed in laying low the Marxist opponent.

At the close of the year of the National Socialist Revolution, therefore, I feel compelled to thank you, my dear Ernst Roehm, for the imperishable services which you have rendered to the National Socialist Movement and the German people, and to assure you how very grateful I am to Fate that I am able to call such men as you my friends and fellow-combatants.

In true (*herzlicher*) friendship and grateful regard,

YOUR ADOLF HITLER.
*Hitler, January 1, 1934* [1c]

lutionism, with which the Storm Troops had identified themselves, was suppressed, but in being driven underground it was made to fill men's minds. No one in the inner circles of the party has any doubt that another opportunity will come for carrying the revolution into its second phase; and no one treats seriously the official explanation of June 30th, that it was a mere expedition for the punishment of homo-sexuals. The brutal ruthlessness and the utter lawlessness of the execution of Röhm were carefully noted by the party for future guidance.

*Hermann Rauschning, 1939* [23d]

## NIGHT OF THE LONG KNIVES

● The lynch justice performed on June 30th, 1934, left an indelible impression not only on the S.A. formations that suffered but on the S.S. lynchers. And the impression was the opposite of that which the leaders intended. Röhm's outspoken revo-

● So far as methods of government and respect for human life and human freedom are concerned Germany has ceased for the time being to be a modern European country. She has reverted to medieval conditions. No pity need be wasted on the dead Nazi leaders, who on every reckoning have richly deserved their fate. So long as they were in authority at the head of the Brown Army they were a menace to

Hitler now had to choose. On one hand, the SA and militants were clamoring for the start of the "second revolution" against the establishment. On the other, the economic power of the country and the army both demanded an end to social disorders and that meant the end of the SA. The latter could offer something Hitler wanted and needed—their endorsement of him for the presidency.

Hitler chose the army and the money lords. The violent reckoning for the SA and others in Hitler's path occurred on June 30, 1934: the "Night of the Long Knives." With the faithful Goebbels at his side, Hitler personally led the operation that captured a

peace and to all orderly progress. That the destruction of these idols of yesterday should give "uniform satisfaction" as a Munich telegram reports, is in accordance with all revolutionary precedent. What is ominously symptomatic of the present state of Germany is the savagery, the disregard for all the forms of law which are the indispensable safeguards of justice and which are sacrosanct in every modern civilized state. What is of still deeper significance is the indifference—even the complacency—with which this resort to the political methods of the Middle Ages is apparently regarded.

The Times (*London*), *July 3, 1934, p. 15*

pierre of the Nazi revolution.

Hitler, like Robespierre, "the incorruptible," has begun to kill. He has sent his bullets against men who, former friends or not, aroused his fanatic moral conscience. Nazis now have begun to kill each other. But Robespierre met the fate he dealt out to his enemies, and today Germany asks where, when and with whom will the killing stop.

No invention of a fiction writer could equal the wildly improbable melodrama of the last 48 hours' events in Germany.

St. Louis Post-Dispatch,
*July 2, 1934, p. 1*

● BERLIN, July 2—Chancellor Hitler has shot his best friend. He has shot the only man in the Nazi party who was intimate enough to call him "thou." Hitler has shot eight of his closest one-time friends. He has shot, too, his most dangerous enemy. Hitler, whom the world called a "softie," whom outsiders thought a "sissy," has become overnight the Robes-

● How many were slain in the purge was never definitely established. In his Reichstag speech of July 13, Hitler announced that sixty-one persons were shot, including nineteen "higher S.A. leaders," that thirteen more died "resisting arrest" and that three "committed suicide"—a total of seventy-seven. *The White Book of the Purge*, published by émigrés in Paris, stated that 401 had been slain, but it iden-

group of SA leaders attending a convention at an Alpine resort south of Munich. In Berlin, Goering and Himmler arrested and shot other SA leaders. Hundreds of people died that one night, purged by the SS and their own leader. The official version maintained this was an emergency measure taken to head off an attempted coup. In actual fact, the victims were certainly not acting like "conspirators" at the moment of the blood bath. Röhm, once Hitler's closest friend, was in bed, drunk, with a male companion. Others were snuffed out while peacefully asleep in their own homes. On July 13, Hitler spoke before the Reichstag, and said that a total of 77 people had died during

tified only 116 of them. At the Munich trial in 1957, the figure of "more than 1,000" was given.

*William L. Shirer, 1960* [24j]

● It was a new role in which Chancellor Hitler appeared yesterday. Although hailed with frantic acclaim in the streets of Berlin, and sure in advance of the hysterical applause of a slavish Reichstag, he was distinctly on the defensive. He spoke as one conscious that he had to justify himself to his own people. Even more significant that that, he was as one standing before the bar of public opinion throughout the whole world. Perhaps never before did so many foreigners wait eagerly for the speech of a German Chancellor. It is safe to say that never before did they get so little from one.

The New York Times, *July 14, 1934, p. 12*

● His [Hitler's] account of the conspiracy was detailed, and his explanation of the wholesale executions was, in effect: "I

am the law and the Supreme Court. I will kill anyone who rises against the state." By comparison Louis XIV's utterance, "I am the state," was mild as a boast of personal power. No such brazening of tyranny had been heard in modern civilization. Mussolini and Stalin are both effective dictators, and have "purged the party" on occasion, but exile, imprisonment and beating have been the extent of their punishments.

*Associated Press, July 15, 1934*

### THE ARMY SWEARS OBEDIENCE

● For the oath which the Armed Forces had taken on August 2, 1934, and which was reaffirmed by law in the following year, was not the mere repetition of the oath to the Constitution which had been sworn under the Republic. It was an oath of personal fealty to Adolf Hitler:

I swear before God to give my unconditional obedience to Adolf Hitler, *Führer* of

Casually dressed, the Führer enjoys a walk in the mountains (December 1937).

the purge. Other sources gave much higher figures.

On August 2, 1934, at the age of 86, President Hindenburg died. Everything was ready for his successor, Adolf Hitler. The offices of President and Chancellor were merged; the new head of Germany would be known as Führer and Reich Chancellor. Hitler had also taken over as Commander in Chief of the Armed Forces, and had the army swear allegiance not to Germany but to him. Henceforth, with the democratic system and domestic opposition to Nazism crushed, the destinies of Adolf Hitler and Germany became one and the same.

the Reich and of the German People, Supreme Commander of the *Wehrmacht,* and I pledge my word as a brave soldier to observe this oath always, even at peril of my life. . . .

. . . At the moment when the Army believed that all opportunities lay open to them, they had made a capitulation infinitely more complete than their surrender to the Allies in the railway compartment in the Forest of Compiègne. Henceforth such opposition as the Army wished to offer to the Nazi régime was no longer in the nature of a struggle with an unscrupulous partner, but of a conspiracy against legitimate and constituted authority, a fact which was to sow the seeds of a harvest of doubt and moral conflict at all levels of the military hierarchy. . . .

. . . By himself assuming the function of War Minister and Supreme Commander of the Armed Forces [Hitler] had translated into starkly practical terms the situa-tion created by the fusion of the Presidency with the Chancellorship four years before, and had given a stiffer twist to the oath which he had exacted from the armed forces. From now on his deputies in the fields of the armed forces and of Foreign Affairs would be men who were not merely subservient to his orders but who thought as he did. For there was no doubt that both Ribbentrop and Keitel were convinced and devoted Nazis at heart.

Above all, the *Führer* had outmanoeuvred, defeated, humiliated, and dragooned the German Army. The armed forces, of which they were but a part, now assumed their position as the third pillar in the structure of the Thousand Year Reich, ranking parallel with, but not above, the Reich Government and the Nazi Party.

*John W. Wheeler-Bennett, 1964* [29b]

# 6

# THE DEMOCRACIES BEGIN TO CRUMBLE

Adolf Hitler now launched his plan for the conquest of Europe. The ruthless format was very clear, amply described in *Mein Kampf*, and reaffirmed in innumerable speeches. The first step was to restore German prestige at the international level, then to bring together in one single Reich all people of German stock, meaning the whole of Austria and the ethnic minorities in Czechoslovakia, Poland, and France.

Finally, the new Reich had to find that "living space" (*Lebensraum*), which, it trumpeted, was essential for its existence. This would be to the detriment of inferior races, that is, Slavs, who occupied such rich, vast territories in Eastern Europe.

In order to implement such a program, it was obvious that Germany had to become a great military power; thus, the two-pronged objective of Hitler's policy. At home, he launched an economic program geared primarily toward accelerating military production. For example, the construction of a "people's automobile" (*Volkswagen*) was announced. Actually industry was intended to turn out, almost exclusively, military vehicles and machinery. Construction of a vast railway and highway network got under way, forerunners of strategic importance in Hitler's rearmament plans. Hitler fully intended to break the Versailles treaty and, under his "guns instead of butter" scheme, to arm Germany. To gain time, he presented to the outside world a picture of a peace-loving, hard-working Germany, concerned solely with raising its standard of living and winning back its old place as a civilized European nation on an equal footing with the other major powers.

England showed little disapproval of a rehabilitated Germany. Historically, it was sea power that made her skittish. France, Germany's traditional foe, did not interfere. Instead, she concentrated on building a large military force and establishing diplomatic relations with several East European countries with an eye toward containing Germany. Mussolini's Fascist

## A FORCE FOR GOOD?

• It is pointless to deny that Hitler succeeded in releasing in the German people a great store of energy and faith in themselves, which had been frustrated during the years of the Depression. The Germans responded to the lead of an authoritarian government which was not afraid to take both risks and responsibility. Thus, to quote only one instance, between January 1933 and December 1934 the number of registered unemployed fell from six millions to two million six hundred thousand, while the number of insured workers employed rose from eleven and a half to fourteen and a half millions. Granted that some measure of economic recovery was general at this time, none the less in Germany it was more rapid and went further than elsewhere, largely as a result of heavy Government expenditure on improving the resources of the country and on public works.

It is natural, therefore, to ask, as many

Germans still ask, whether there was not some point up to which the Nazi movement was a force for good, but after which its original idealism became corrupted. Whatever truth there may be in this, so far as it is a question of the rank and file of the movement, so far as Hitler and the Nazi leadership are concerned, this is a view contradicted by the evidence. For all the evidence points to the opposite view, namely, that from the first Hitler and the other Nazi leaders thought in terms solely of power, their own power, and the power of the nation over which they ruled.

In a secret memorandum of 3 May 1935, Dr. Schacht, the man who had the greatest responsibility for Germany's economic recovery, wrote: 'The accomplishment of the armament programme with speed and in quantity is *the* problem of German politics, and everything else should be subordinated to this purpose, as long as the main purpose is not imperilled by neglecting all other questions.'

*Alan Bullock, 1962* [41]

Hitler Youth (July 1936). This vast Nazi organization provided military, athletic, and ideological training to boys and girls between the ages of 6 and 18.

## THE FIGHT FOR SPACE

• If you do not give us space on this earth then we ourselves will take this space. That is why we are National Socialists. We fight for the vital rights of our people in this world. The blood of millions can be pledged only if they know that the conflict does not serve a particular class, but that it benefits the entire people. Do not believe that this people will go to war again, if it does not carry a different conviction to the battlefield than it did formerly. The day will come when the German people will rise up and break their bonds asunder, when in millions of hearts there will be one single faith, one embracing conviction. We do not fight for the German middle class, nor for the German proletariat; we fight for our people, for wife and child, we fight for our children's children.

I am happy that fate guided me, a simple soldier for four years, through the hell of blood and fire. I cannot imagine that a true German would ever take the respon-

sibility of leading his people through this hell a second time unless he was convinced that from this inferno a paradise would be forthcoming for his people.

*Hitler, April 9, 1927* [22q]

• For centuries the cry of our forefathers has rung out: Give us space! . . . The German people is crowded together on a hopelessly small area. He who looks into the future must reach the shocking conclusion that we, as a result of the size of our territory, are destined to extinction as a people if a change is not forthcoming in the relationship of the soil and population.

*Hitler, November 21, 1927* [22r]

• If ever in the future of Germany the sword must be drawn, then not for any dream-like visions or any sort of crazy phantasies. If the sword must be drawn, then it must be drawn in the service of the plow—that is, for German soil—so that

Italy eyed the role of Hitler's party in Germany with sympathy.

With the political climate favorable, Hitler made an overt move. In October of 1933, he withdrew Germany from the League of Nations after a squabble with France. For Hitler, 1934 was a year of both success and failure. He engineered the assassination of Austria's head of state, but the ensuing putsch that would have extended his power failed. Temporarily, Austria eluded him. But this also was the year he defied the Versailles treaty by expanding the German army from the permissible 100,000 to 700,000 men, and laid the groundwork for the German air force, the Luftwaffe. The World War I Allies

some day the time will come when the sword will again become the plow.
*Hitler, March 1928* [22s]

### PEACE & FRIENDSHIP

● The German people do not want war. On the contrary, because the German people loves peace, it fights for its vital rights and champions the conditions necessary for the existence of our nation of 65,000,-000. Germany and the German people have no reason to desire a war in order to reestablish the honor of the nation and the honor of its men and soldiers. Our goal is to make our people happy again by assuring them daily bread. This is a tremendous task, and the world, therefore, should leave us in peace.
*Hitler, October 22, 1933* [22t]

**Berlin, 1936: Adolf Hitler enters the Olympic Stadium as thousands watch.**

An SA rally in Berlin.

let him.

In 1936, Hitler played his most dangerous hand in the political game, moving German troops back into the Rhineland, which had been demilitarized after the Treaty of Versailles. The only noise heard was a formal rumble of official protest. France, with her supposedly impregnable Maginot Line, mobilized a few divisions along the border while the Germans held their breath. Neither side opened fire.

Hitler celebrated his triumph regally before the whole world at the 1936 Olympic Games in Berlin. Once again, Germany was a major power, and a new alignment was taking shape in

● We assure the world that the German Government and the German people have only one wish: To live in peace and friendship with all nations in order to be able to finish their internal reconstruction.
*Hitler, November 6, 1933* [22u]

### HITLER'S STYLE

● Of all the speakers who have recently appeared before German crowds, Hitler is probably the most indomitable fighter. For an hour, two hours, he will stand on the platform, an inspired preacher, occasionally enlivening his arguments with witty remarks; a man with ideas, who is easy to listen to, but—it must be confessed—who is also at times apt to act as a soporific. But then he becomes inspired again. His figure shoots up and down on the platform; his arms saw the air in gestures that, though they are poor miming and do not illustrate what is said, do excellently convey the speaker's emotions, and infect the listeners with them. When during a recriminatory speech Hitler pecks at the audience with his forefinger like a bird of prey, each and every member of it feels personally responsible for the sins of the German nation.

The result is that the man on the platform no longer discusses anything, but gives battle. The masses do not see the enemy; they do not realize that the fighter has the enemy within himself. He is fighting against the disintegration of the nation, against the political indolence of the masses, against the culpable negligences of men who have been set in authority— and in reality he is fighting against the Marxist that was once himself, against the lazy schoolboy, against the irresolute man who missed his opportunity in 1922, was twice defeated in 1923, did not take power when he had the chance in 1930, and missed it in 1932. He is fighting against his own fear, against his private devil like an anchorite of old. He is no longer an agitator, nor is he indulging in oratorical exercises; this is exorcism. Hence he can say what he likes—even if it were that the moon is made of green

Europe. On the one hand, there was the Rome-Berlin axis, consolidated after the Italian venture in Ethiopia and the outbreak of civil war in Spain. On the other, France had formed alliances with Poland, the Soviet Union, and Czechoslovakia. Then there was England, trying to maintain a doubtul, shifting equilibrium. There were no major jolts through 1937. It almost seemed as though the policy of appeasement with the restless Fascist regimes had been successful. But one day in November, 1937, Hitler decided to move ahead with the second phase of his grandiose program. In a secret meeting, he informed his collaborators of the deadlines before turning to the next phase

cheese—and the audience will applaud. When bombs are falling, nobody troubles to see whether they are painted grey or green. . . .

*Konrad Heiden, 1935,* [9b]

● . . . Hitler says "Jew," and everyone understands. Again and again the truth is forgotten that the masses—to which, as we know, even the most cultured person belongs if he is one of thousands—would rather hear lying facts than truthful arguments; and that if a lying fact is repeated often enough, they believe it wholeheartedly—a "tremendous, almost incredible result," which even a Hitler notes "with amazement."

*Konrad Heiden, 1936* [101]

### REARMAMENT OF GERMANY

● 'In those days [1918] the situation seemed hopeless. It appeared even more desperate if one remained as firmly convinced as I was that "Versailles" could not represent the end', wrote Gustav Krupp von Bohlen und Halbach, the adopted head of the dynasty, in proud remembrance in 1941. 'If ever there should be a resurrection for Germany, if ever she were to shake off the chains of Versailles, then Krupps would have to be prepared. The machines were demolished; the tools were destroyed; but one thing remained— the men, the men at the drawing boards and in the workshops, who, in happy cooperation had brought the manufacture of guns to its last perfection. Their skill would have to be saved, their immense resources of knowledge and experience. Even though camouflaged I had to maintain Krupps as an armament factory for the distant future, in spite of all obstacles.'

Thus the great armament industry was temporarily 'converted' into an arsenal of peace, devoted to the manufacture of articles which seemed to be particularly remote from the activities of the weaponsmithy. 'Even the Allied spying commission was fooled', Krupp adds proudly: 'padlocks, milk cans, cash registers, railmending machines, refuse carts and sim-

of his war-bound policy.

Austria was the first European country to fall into Hitler's hands. This time, his call for Anschluss (union) was not an improvised maneuver, as it had been in 1934, but one that had been worked out to the last detail with the Nazis "fifth column" (Austrian collaborators) in Vienna.

Now that the Rome-Berlin axis was thoroughly consolidated, there was little or no chance for the Austrian government to maneuver. The situation came to a head early in 1938 with the discovery in Vienna of a Nazi plot to seize power. Austrian Chancellor Kurt von Schuschnigg requested a conference with

ilar rubbish appeared really innocent, and locomotives and motor cars appeared perfectly "peaceful".'

*John W. Wheeler-Bennett, 1964* [29c]

• I do not support the rearmament of the German people for the reason that I am a share-holder. I believe that I am perhaps the only statesman in the world who does not have a bank account. I hold no shares; I have no share in any kind of an enterprise; I draw no dividends. What I want, however, is that my people should become strong so that they can endure in this world. That is my will! . . .

German people! Behold the greatness and the totality of the last three years! Be fair. Do you, if you are a decent German, have reason, before the German people, before history and before posterity, to be ashamed during the last three years? Do you not finally have reason to be proud again? Are you not able to say again: Lord God, whatever the situation may perhaps be here and there, for the most part we have once more become a re-

spectable people! We have also become a very industrious and energetic people. . . . In these three years we have proved that we are a people which need not be ashamed before others. I do not subordinate myself to the world, for the world cannot judge me. I subject myself only to you, German people!

*Hitler, March 27, 1936* [22v]

• . . . the biggest single factor in the recovery of confidence and faith in Germany was the sense of this power, a renewed confidence and faith in 'the German mission', expressed in an increasingly aggressive nationalism which had little use for the rights of other, less powerful nations. The psychology of Nazism, no less than Nazi economics, was one of preparation for war. Both depended for their continued success upon the maintenance of a national spirit and a national effort which in the end must find expression in aggressive action. War, the belief in violence and the right of the stronger, were not corruptions of Nazism, they were its es-

Hitler, and the two met on February 12 at Berchtesgaden.

Hitler issued an ultimatum. Either the Austrian government cede power to the Nazis or the troops of the Reich would invade. Schuschnigg had little choice, but he played a surprise card. On March 8, he called for a plebiscite to allow the Austrian people to decide their fate. Hitler, amazed and furious, threatened to invade immediately. Schuschnigg was forced to resign. But Austrian president Wilhelm Miklas resisted German demands that he name the Austrian Nazi Seyss-Inquart to the chancellorship. Finally he capitulated, hoping to avoid bloodshed and total domination by Germany. But it was too late;

A torchlight parade of Nazi leaders (August 1938).

German troops had already crossed the border between Germany and Austria—at the "request" of Seyss-Inquart and with the endorsement of Mussolini. And so, on March 12, 1938, Hitler made his first foreign conquest.

Later that day, Hitler marched in triumph into his native land. Cheering crowds greeted him in every village—it was a great personal triumph for him. In a speech in Linz, he said: "If Providence once called me forth from this town to be the leader of the Reich, it must in so doing have charged me with a mission, and that mission could only be to restore my dear homeland to the German Reich. I have believed in this mission, I

sence. Anyone who visited Germany in 1936–7 needed to be singularly blind not to see the ends to which all this vast activity was directed.

*Alan Bullock, 1962* [41]

## ENTERING THE RHINELAND

● . . . even later, when he was waging war against almost the entire world, [Hitler] always termed the remilitarization of the Rhineland the most daring of all his undertakings. "We had no army worth mentioning; at that time it would not even have had the fighting strength to maintain itself against the Poles. If the French had taken any action, we would have been easily defeated; our resistance would have been over in a few days. And what air force we had then was ridiculous. A few Junkers 52's from Lufthansa, and not even enough bombs for them."

*Albert Speer, 1969* [25a]

## THE ATTRACTION OF NAZISM

● The German conception of politics had always been infected with aesthetics, and Nazism gave a central place to this quality. One of the reasons for the Weimar Republic's failure was that its representatives did not understand the German psychology and thought of politics solely as politics. It remained for Hitler to endow public affairs with the necessary éclat. This he did by his endless obfuscations, his theatrical scenarios, the storms of ecstasy and idolization. Those vaults created by massed searchlight beams were the fitting symbol for it all: walls of magic and light erected against the dark menace of the outside world. And if the Germans did not share Hitler's hunger for space, his anti-Semitism, his vulgar and brutal qualities, they applauded him and followed him because he had once more restored passion to politics, and overlaid it with a note of dire significance.

*Joachim C. Fest, 1973* [61]

Hitler's entry into Vienna in March 1938 was triumphal—quite unlike his earlier entry as a youth in 1907,

● One word . . . on the simplest and most elementary, but perhaps most effective and most characteristic method of domination employed by National Socialism—the marching. At first this marching seemed to be a curious whim of the National Socialists. These eternal night marches, this keeping of the whole population on the march, seemed to be a senseless waste of time and energy. Only much later was there revealed in it a subtle intention based on a well-judged adjustment of ends and means. Marching diverts men's thoughts. Marching kills thought. Marching makes an end of individuality. Marching is the indispensable magic stroke performed in order to accustom the people to a mechanical, quasi-ritualistic activity until it becomes second nature.

*Hermann Rauschning, 1939* [23e]

## THE DAZZLING RALLIES

● . . . The Nuremberg rallies held every year in September were masterpieces of theatrical art, with the most carefully devised effects. 'I had spent six years in St. Petersburg before the war in the best days of the old Russian ballet,' wrote Sir Nevile Henderson, 'but for grandiose beauty I have never seen a ballet to compare with it.' To see the films of the Nuremberg rallies even today is to be recaptured by the hypnotic effect of thousands of men marching in perfect order, the music of the massed bands, the forest of standards and flags, the vast perspectives of the stadium, the smoking torches, the dome of searchlights. The sense of power, of force and unity was irresistible, and all converged with a mounting crescendo of excitement on the supreme moment when the Führer himself made his entry. Paradoxically, the man who was most affected by such spectacles was their originator, Hitler himself, and, as Rosenberg remarks in his memoirs, they played an indispensable part in the process of self-intoxication.

*Alan Bullock,*
*1962* [4k]

have lived and fought for it, and I believe I have now fulfilled it." [24u]

The next day the Austrian government issued a decree that began: "Austria is a province of the German Reich. . . ."

Austria had gone down without a shot being fired. Hitler turned next toward Czechoslovakia. The European powers had not interfered with his annexation of Austria, but the Czech democracy posed a riskier problem. Hitler could count on the backing of Italy, Hungary, and Poland, with whom he had signed a 10-year treaty in 1934. But could he count on appeasement from the major powers pledged to back Czechoslovakia

The foreign press viewed with alarm Hitler's proclamation of Anschluss and decried his use of trickery and armed force in Austria.

## THE 1936 OLYMPICS

• A Nazi-saluting, German-singing crowd of 110,000 last Saturday watched the opening ceremony featured by the shortest speech that Hitler ever made. (Rules limit the official who raises the Olympic curtain to a formal statement of sixteen words.)

Newsweek, *August 8, 1936, p. 32*

• Each of the German victories—and there were a surprising number of these—made [Hitler] happy, but he was highly annoyed by the series of triumphs by the marvelous colored American runner, Jesse Owens. People whose antecedents came from the jungle were primitive, Hitler said with a shrug; their physiques were stronger than those of civilized whites. They represented unfair competition and hence must be excluded from future games. Hitler was also jolted by the jubilation of the Berliners when the French team filed solemnly into the Olympic Stadium. They had marched

—Great Britain, France, and the Soviet Union?

Hitler's pretext was a sizable German minority in Czechoslovakia's Sudetenland, which, he insisted, was being abused and murdered. Czech President Eduard Beneš tried to negotiate with Hitler, but on September 7, 1938, Germany broke off all negotiations, citing alleged excesses by Czech police.

Great Britain's Prime Minister, Neville Chamberlain, urgently requested a meeting with Hitler and, on September 15 at Berchtesgaden, Hitler proposed that Britain and France agree to a secession of the Sudentenland, based on the right of self-determination. A week later the two men met again, this time in

past Hitler with raised arms and thereby sent the crowd into transports of enthusiasm. But in the prolonged applause Hitler sensed a popular mood, a longing for peace and reconciliation with Germany's western neighbor. If I am correctly interpreting Hitler's expression at the time, he was more disturbed than pleased by the Berliners' cheers.

*Albert Speer, 1969* [25b]

● Original German theory to explain Negro sport supremacy, prematurely evolved before the Schmeling-Louis prizefight, was that Negroes are not really people. Last week, Realmleader Adolf Hitler conspicuously neglected to invite Negro winners up to shake hands with him in his box, and Nazi newspapers invented an even more facile excuse for Germany's feeble showing of only three winners . . . in the men's track and field events by describing the Negroes who between them won half the U.S. total as "a black auxiliary force."

Time, *August 17, 1936, p. 37–38*

**ROME-BERLIN AXIS**

● Out of the mutuality of the Fascist and the National Socialist Revolutions there has arisen today an association not only of views but of action. This is a stroke of good fortune in an age and for the world when the tendencies of destruction and deformation are visible everywhere. Fascist Italy has become a new empire through the able and creative activity of a man of organizing genius. You, Benito Mussolini, with your own eyes will have been able to establish this fact in connection with our National Socialist State; Germany, too, in her national attitude and in her military strength has again become a world power. . . .

. . . Every attempt to separate or to dissolve such a community of peoples by playing them off one against the other through suspicions or through the attributions of false aims will fail. It will fail because of the desire of the 115,000,000 who in this hour form this demonstration, and especially because of the will of the

Godesberg, and Hitler upped his demands. The Czech government refused to accept the proposals. France, headed by Premier Edouard Daladier, and Britain agreed that they would have to honor their commitments to Czechoslovakia. At a rally in Berlin, on the evening of September 26, Hitler insisted that the Sudetenland would have to be annexed by the Reich by October 1st—"I have made an offer to Mr. Beneš that is nothing else than a realization of what he himself has already conceded. He now holds the decision in his hand. Peace or war! Either he will now accept this offer and at last give the Germans their freedom, or we will take this freedom for our-

"The Lion's Share"—a Soviet impression of the Munich Agreement.

L-R: Mussolini, Hitler, Daladier, and, in the background, Chamberlain (Sept. 29, 1938).

selves!" [22y]

But the French and Czech troops massing on the borders outnumbered the Germans. Also, the German generals disapproved of Hitler's intentions, and the German people were apathetic to the supposed offenses against Germany by the Czechs. Hitler wrote to Chamberlain, leaving it to him to "bring the Government in Prague to reason." The stage was set for Munich, where, to prevent war, Chamberlain, Daladier, Hitler, and Mussolini signed the Munich Agreement, which gave Germany the Sudetenland. Chamberlain returned to London, debarked from his airplane, and spoke of "peace in our time."

two men who stand here before you and speak to you.

*Hitler, September 28, 1937* [22w]

### THE RIGHT TO SELF-DETERMINATION

● Over 10,000,000 Germans live in two of the states adjoining our frontiers. Till 1866 they were constitutionally united with the whole German people. They fought up to 1918 in the Great War shoulder to shoulder with the German soldiers of the Reich. Under the terms of the peace they were kept against their will from forming a union with the Reich. This in itself is sufficiently distressing. There can, however, be no doubt about one thing. The fact that they are now citizens of other states does not deprive them of their natural rights as members of a national community. A peope has the right to self-determination, as we were solemnly assured in Wilson's Fourteen Points which served as the basis of the Armistice; this cannot be overlooked simply because the people in question happen to be Germans! In the long run it is intolerable for a self-respecting world power to know that across the frontier are kinsmen who have to suffer severe persecution simply because of their sympathy, their feeling of union, and their common point of view with the whole German people.

*Hitler, February 20, 1938* [22x]

### SHOWDOWN IN AUSTRIA

● Today it seems to me providential that Fate should have chosen Braunau on the Inn as my birthplace. For this little town lies on the boundary between two German states which we of the younger generation at least have made it our life work to reunite by every means at our disposal.

German-Austria must return to the great German mother country, and not because of any economic considerations. No, and again no: even if such a union were un-

American cartoonist D. R. Fitzpatrick observes that Hitler still seeks more *lebensraum* after the dismemberment of Czechoslovakia.

important from an economic point of view; yes, even if it were harmful, it must nevertheless take place. One blood demands one Reich. Never will the German nation possess the moral right to engage in colonial politics until, at least, it embraces its own sons within a single state.
*Hitler, 1924* [111]

• Fascists capered joyfully from their homes. Great crowds howling "One Reich, One People!" tramped through the narrow, twisted streets around old St. Stephen's Cathedral, their flushed faces glowing in the light of torches. Others . . . chased Jews about the Leopoldstadt ghetto section, crying; "Hop the twig, Judah! (hang yourself)." Police suddenly blossomed with Swastika armbands, and shopkeepers ran out of brown cloth. Jews and monarchists . . . frantically sought places on outgoing trains. Three babies born in Vienna hospitals were named Adolf. . . .

. . . Austria's extinction spread alarm and impotent rage throughout Europe. For five years the buffer state's red and white standard had fluttered as a barricade against Hitler's vaulting dream of expansion.

The problem of keeping Germany's talons off Austria was a major worry to Britain, France, and Italy long before anyone considered Adolf Hitler more than a moonstruck crank. The ex-Allies made Berlin agree to respect Vienna's independence in Article 80 of the Versailles Treaty, signed June 28, 1919. When, less than two months later, Germany promulgated its first constitution, with a loophole for *Anschluss* (union with Austria), the three powers protested and the clause came out. Dead set against a revival of German expansionist dreams, they paid heavily from then on to support the economically unsound Danubian republic.
Newsweek, *March 21, 1938, p. 15–17*

## AGREEING TO SECESSION

• Premier Daladier and his Foreign Minister, Georges Bonnet, arrived in London on September 18, for consultations with

Hitler inspects the guard of honour in Prague's Hradschin Castle (March 15, 1939).

Hitler's troops entered the Sudetenland on October 1 and occupation was complete by October 10. The army had taken over all the fortifications along the border and a large section of territory. Once again, not a shot was fired.

It is not surprising that Hitler's appetite was not sated and, in view of the Anglo-French appeasement of his every move, his next step was predictable. He wanted all of Czechoslovakia. On the night of March 14-15, 1939, after a stormy session in Berlin with Beneš, he got it. On the afternoon of March 15, German troops marched into Prague. Hitler himself was there on March 16 to proclaim the Slovakian, Bohemian, and Moravian prov-

the British cabinet. No thought was given to bringing the Czechs in. The British and the French, anxious to avoid war at any cost, lost little time in agreeing on joint proposals which the Czechs would have to accept. All territories inhabited more than 50 per cent by Sudeten Germans must be turned over to Germany to assure "the maintenance of peace and the safety of Czechoslovakia's vital interests." In return Britain and France agreed to join in "an international guarantee of the new boundaries . . . against unprovoked aggression." Such a guarantee would supplant the mutual-assistance treaties which the Czech state had with France and Russia. This was an easy way out for the French, and led by Bonnet, who, as the course of events would show, was determined to outdo Chamberlain in the appeasement of Hitler, they seized upon it.

*William L. Shirer, 1960* [24k]

● On its face, the London settlement must be profoundly disillusioning to the world—that part of the world which still clings to the democratic principle. It looks like abject surrender to the dictator of an even more powerful Germany. The hope arises that, in the minds of Messrs. Chamberlain and Daladier there are considerations that are not apparent to those of us who are 3,000 miles from the scene. Certainly, they must have felt that the immediate alternative—if the Sudeten cession were denied—was the possibility of mass slaughter.

The lesson to the United States is clear. However keenly we may feel about Europe, our first duty is to ourselves. We must find a solution of our more serious economic difficulties. We must look to our military and naval defenses.

*St. Louis Post-Dispatch, September 19, 1938, p. 2c*

### HITLER VERSUS BENEŠ

● . . . : The tragedy of Benes is that he lived to speak the word that partitions and

inces as protectorates of the German Reich. Czechoslovakia had disappeared from the map of Europe.

Hitler's next target was Poland, but it seemed unlikely that country could be engulfed without a fight. More than willing to let the powers continue to appease him, he tried a tactic that had proved successful in the past. He launched a vigorous propaganda campaign, charging ill treatment of German minorities in Poland and the Free City of Danzig.

Britain and France were no longer inclined to play the role of "procurer," as they had done with Hitler's lust for Czechoslovakia. As 1938 ended and in the first half of 1939, positions

perhaps dissolves the state he worked with Masaryk to create. At the end the decision he made was inescapable, and the only crumb of comfort left to him on this dark day is that he surrendered under pressure in the name of peace, brought to bear on his friends and the cosponsors of the synthesis that until now they encouraged him to defend.

There is not much comfort for the rest of us in that reflection. There is not much comfort in the thought that in the historic week between Mr. Chamberlain's visit to Berchtesgaden and his visit to Godesberg the price of peace has been raised by Hitler. If demands for the secession of other minorities in Czechoslovakia are not raised today on the Rhine, it will be only because the satisfaction of these claims is postponed as other claims come crowding in.

The New York Times, *September 22, 1938, p. 22*

to those of us who listened in amazement to his mad outburst at the jammed Sportpalast in Berlin. Shouting and shrieking in the worst paroxysm I had ever seen him in, he venomously hurled personal insults at "Herr Beneš," declared that the issue of war or peace was now up to the Czech President and that, in any case, he would have the Sudetenland by October 1. Carried away as he was by his angry torrent of words and the ringing cheers of the crowd, he was shrewd enough to throw a sop to the British Prime Minister. He thanked him for his efforts for peace and reiterated that this was his last territorial claim in Europe. "We want no Czechs" he muttered contemptuously.

*William L. Shirer, 1960* [241]

## SURRENDER AT MUNICH

• That evening [September 26, 1938] Hitler burned his bridges, or so it seemed

• The conferees got down to business when Mussolini, speaking third in turn—

shifted and began to harden.

The Allies saw the "Pact of Steel" between Germany and Italy formalized on May 22, 1939—the alliance that became known as the Rome-Berlin Axis. Francisco Franco, who had been aided by German officers, weapons, and airplanes during the Spanish Civil War, also sided with Hitler.

Britain and France reaffirmed their solidarity with Poland. They were supported by the United States, which was becoming alarmed at the aggressive policies of Germany and, incidentally, of Japan.

The major question mark was the Soviet Union, which felt

Daladier was left to the last—said that "in order to bring about a practical solution of the problem" he had brought with him a definite written proposal. Its origins are interesting and remained unknown to Chamberlain, I believe, to his death. From the memoirs of François-Poncet and Henderson it is obvious that they too were ignorant of them. In fact, the story only became known long after the violent deaths of the two dictators.

What the Duce now fobbed off as his own compromise plan had been hastily drafted the day before in the German Foreign Office in Berlin by Goering, Neurath and Weizsaecker behind the back of Foreign Minister von Ribbentrop, whose judgment the three men did not trust. Goering took it to Hitler, who said it might do, and then it was hurriedly translated into French by Dr. Schmidt and passed along to the Italian ambassador, Attolico, who telephoned the text of it to the Italian dictator in Rome just before he entrained for Munich. Thus it was that the "Italian proposal," which provided the informal conference not only with its sole

agenda but with the basic terms which eventually became the Munich Agreement, were in fact German proposals concocted in Berlin.

This must have seemed fairly obvious from the text, which closely followed Hitler's rejected Godesberg demands; but it was not obvious to Daladier and Chamberlain or to their ambassadors in Berlin, who now attended them. The Premier, according to the German minutes, "welcomed the Duce's proposal and declared that he himself had conceived a solution on the lines of this proposal." As for Ambassador Henderson, as he later wrote, he thought Mussolini "had tactfully put forward as his own a combination of Hitler's and the Anglo-French proposals"; while Ambassador François-Poncet got the impression that the conferees were working on a British memorandum "drawn up by Horace Wilson." [83] So easily were the British and French statesmen and diplomats, bent on appeasement at any cost, deceived!

*William L. Shirer, 1960* [24m]

At the front: Hitler confers with his generals (1939).

The peace of Munich was a peace at the expense of liberty. It boded ill for the future and for the cause of freedom. Any peace, to be lasting, must be based not on force but on justice. Now justice must be buttressed by force—a greater force than the dictators could command.

*Sir Archibald Sinclair, M.P.,*
The Times (*London*), October 20, 1938

## THE OCCUPATION OF THE SUDETENLAND

Hitler's prestige rose to new heights in Germany, where relief that war had been avoided was combined with delight in the gains that had been won on the cheap. Whether those who opposed a policy of risking war would ever have carried out their plan to seize Hitler—as General Halder and others subsequently claimed—remains uncertain; but Hitler's success, without war, cut the ground away from under their feet.

Abroad the effect was equally startling, and Mr. Churchill described the results of the Munich settlement in a famous speech on 5 October 1938:

At Berchtesgaden . . . £1 was demanded at the pistol's point. When it was given (at Godesberg), £2 was demanded at the pistol's point. Finally the Dictator consented to take £1 17s. 6d. and the rest in promises of goodwill for the future. . . . We are in the presence of a disaster of the first magnitude.

*Alan Bullock, 1962* [4m]

In *Mein Kampf*, Hitler wrote that the worst of crimes was to leave things unfinished; he harshly condemned *die Halbheit* or half measures. What he called half measures others would term moderation.

In this he represented an outstanding trait in the German character. Germans go to extremes. They want everything immediately; like spoiled brats they are annoyed, and they feel wronged, if they are not given forthwith what they crave. No sooner have they made one gain than they are obsessed by the lust to make another. Not knowing when and where to stop has ever been the cause of Germany's successive defeats.

*André François-Poncet, 1946* [7c]

threatened by Germany and had been excluded from the Anglo-French sellout at Munich. Now the Western powers were interested in wooing the Eastern giant, but so was Adolf Hitler. Soviet dictator Josef Stalin seemed in an enviable position, but only he knew how militarily weak the U.S.S.R. really was. Stalin chose, and on August 23, 1939, a Russo-German Non-Aggression Treaty was signed in Moscow. Joachim von Ribbentrop, Hitler's Minister of Foreign Affairs, signed for Germany. Stalin had bought time and, along the way, a parcel of Poland to be delivered after Hitler invaded that land. Stalin was not the only one interested in buying time. Hitler told his military chiefs on

## ALLIANCE WITH RUSSIA? NO!

• I consider Bolshevism the most malignant poison that can be given to a people. I do not want my own people, therefore, to come into contact with this teaching. As a citizen of this nation I myself shall not do what I should have to condemn my fellow citizens for doing. I demand from every German workman that he shall not have any relations with these international mischief-makers and he shall never see me clinking glasses or rubbing shoulders with them. Moreover, any further treaty connections with the present Bolshevik Russia would be completely worthless for us. It is out of the question to think that National Socialist Germany should ever be bound to protect Bolshevism, or that we, on our side, should ever agree to accept the assistance of a Bolshevik State. For I fear that the moment any nation should agree to accept such assistance, it would thereby seal its own doom.

*Hitler, January 30, 1937* [22z]

## ALLIANCE WITH RUSSIA? YES!

• After supper [on August 21, 1939] Hitler called his entourage together. "We are going to conclude a nonaggression pact with Russia. Here, read this. A telegram from Stalin." It briefly acknowledged the agreement that had been reached. To see the names of Hitler and Stalin linked in friendship on a piece of paper was the most staggering, the most exciting turn of events I could possibly have imagined. . . .

Goebbels held an evening press conference on August 23 in which he offered commentary on the pact. Hitler telephoned him immediately afterward. He wanted to know how the foreign correspondents had reacted. With eyes glistening feverishly, he told us what Goebbels had said. "The sensation was fantastic. And when the church bells simultaneously began ringing outside, a British correspondent fatalistically remarked: 'That is the death knell of the British Empire.'" These words made the strongest impres-

August 22, the day before the formal signing of the agreement, "My pact is only meant to stall for time, gentlemen. We will crush the Soviet Union."

Hitler's confrontation with the enormity of the Soviet battle-ground was for the future, however, and now Der Führer was free to act in the matter of Poland. Neither Britain's reaffirmation of her pact with Poland nor Mussolini's message that he could not possibly come immediately to Hitler's aid deterred him. He ignored the tacit disapproval of many high-ranking Nazis and his own generals, who feared Anglo-French strength. The diplomatic initiatives he took in late August, ostensibly

sion upon Hitler in his euphoria that night. He thought he now stood so high as to be out of the reach of fate.

*Albert Speer, 1969* [25c]

• LONDON, Aug. 21—The deadliest high explosives could not have caused more damage in London than the news late tonight that the Nazi and Soviet governments had agreed on a non-aggression pact behind the backs of the British and French military missions in Moscow.

Anger and stupefaction were the first reactions here. They were all the more intense because neither of the Western Governments appeared to have had any inkling of what was impending. It will take some time for the smoke to clear away, but when it does the diplomatic picture may well be changed beyond all recognition.

*Ferdinand Kuhn, Jr., in* The New York Times, *August 22, 1939, p. 1*

• The British-French policy ever since

Hitler began to "right the wrongs" of Versailles has been utterly unrealistic. The democracies stood by and watched another democracy die in Spain. They sold out Czechoslovakia. They have never been willing to say "halt" and, as Robert Dell, veteran observer of European affairs writes . . . they could have said that word to Hitler and presumably have made it stick at any point.

Why did they choose appeasement instead? Because the Chamberlain choice was Hitler on the Rhine rather than the risk of Communism. The Chamberlain government hoped that it might have Russian help in the vent of war, but it refused, at least until recently, to sit down at the table with Russia in time of peace.

The European nightmare of rapprochement between Fascist totalitarianism and Communist totalitarianism has taken actual form. . . .

Like him or not, Hitler has made dunces of Chamberlain and Daladier; he has outsmarted Europe in a dazzling coup d'état.

St. Louis Post Dispatch, *August 22, 1939, p. 2c*

# Bluebeard's Wife

Nonaggression pact with the USSR: Hitler got what he wanted.

Another viewpoint: Stalin felt he got the better end of the deal.

with the objective of softening the British and Polish attitudes, served mainly as a smokescreen to disguise military preparations for a plan decided on the previous April. On August 31, German Gestapo agents fabricated several incidents along the Polish border, to provide a trumped-up provocation.

On September 1, 1939, at 5:45 A.M., Hitler invaded Poland. On September 3, 1939, Great Britain and France declared war on Germany. World War II had begun. "If any nations are to be ruined," said Hitler, "it will certainly not be the German nation. We are fighting for our rights. We have no desire for war. We have been attacked." [22cc]

• Whatever the agreement means, it is not peace; it serves only to aggravate the crisis. War is not inevitable until the armies get the signal to march, and even at this last moment it still seems unbelievable that any human being should be so lost to all sense of human responsibility as to give that fatal command.

The New York Times, *August 24, 1939, p. 18*

• Hitler had told me . . . his view of the value of treaties. He was ready, he said, to sign anything. He was ready to guarantee any frontier and to conclude a nonaggression pact with anyone. It was a simpleton's idea not to avail oneself of expedients of this sort because the day might come when some formal agreement would have to be broken. Every pact sworn to was broken or became out of date sooner or later. Anyone who was so fussy that he had to consult his conscience about whether he could keep to a pact, whatever the pact and whatever the situation, was a fool.

*Hermann Rauschning, 1939* [23t]

## WAR IS DECLARED

• Adolf Hitler has his war, and Adolf Hitler must be destroyed.

This man's destruction is the first order of business on civilised Europe's program.

St. Louis Post-Dispatch
*September 1, 1939, p. 2c*

• . . . how vividly I remember the contrast between the wild enthusiasm of 1914 and the abysmal despondency of 1939— and something akin to consternation in our immediate entourage.

I was in the Chancellery at the time, and I saw Hitler for a brief moment. . . . He was sitting slumped in his chair, deep in thought, a look of incredulity and baffled chagrin on his face.

*Heinrich Hoffmann, 1955* [14c]

• One really wonders on what grounds the English had the insolence to declare war on the Axis Powers.

*Goebbels, February 2, 1942* [18a]

# 7
# WORLD WAR II

When Hitler left Berlin to join his general staff at the front, the crowd did not applaud.

In Poland, the defending army mounted its crack troops on horseback, but they could do little against German planes and the blitzkrieg (lightning war) of tanks and well-armed, well-trained men. Within 30 days, Warsaw had fallen and Poland disappeared into the Nazi maw. The Soviet Union collected its slice.

The first months of the war were quiet. It was called the "phony war" and Hitler's deputies mouthed phony offers of peace. In April, Hitler struck suddenly at the north, at Denmark and Norway. In May, he pointed his troops west, at the Netherlands, Belgium, and France, claiming that the low countries were plotting with the Allies to invade the Reich. The panzer divisions rolled menacingly across the fields. Tanks and screaming dive bombers slashed at enemy soldiers and civilians alike.

The French, who had been waiting for an invasion from the direction of Germany, hurriedly shifted to the north the divisions that were sitting behind the Maginot Line. But the operations of German armored divisions on the Somme-Aisne line were lightning-swift. Only two days after the first attack by Hitler's panzers, the French first line of defense was shattered. The Germans forged ahead toward the north coast, encountering virtually no resistance. In his field headquarters in the west, Hitler, who was directing the advance, was jubilant. He had sent his armies against the French, he declared, to teach them "an historic lesson." A large part of the French army and the British expeditionary force was cut off by the advancing Germans in the fields of Flanders. In one of the most magnificent exploits of the war, the troops were evacuated at Dunkerque by thousands of ships, large and small, that streamed across the English Channel from Britain.

On June 10, four days before the fall of Paris, Italy entered

Hitler and a group of his generals inspect the German front near Warsaw (September 1939).

On a beach near Dunkirk, British troops wait to be evacuated (June 1940).

## FRANCE'S DOWNFALL

• "HERE ON THE ELEVENTH OF NOVEMBER 1918 SUCCUMBED THE CRIMINAL PRIDE OF THE GERMAN EMPIRE—VANQUISHED BY THE FREE PEOPLES WHICH IT TRIED TO ENSLAVE."

Hitler reads it and Goering reads it. They all read it, standing there in the June sun and the silence. I look for the expression in Hitler's face. I am but fifty yards from him and see him through my glasses as though he were directly in front of me. I have seen that face many times at the great moments of his life. But today! It is afire with scorn, anger, hate, revenge, triumph.

He steps off the monument and contrives to make even this gesture a masterpiece of contempt. He glances back at it, contemptuous, angry—angry, you almost feel, because he cannot wipe out the awful, provoking lettering with one sweep of his high Prussian boot. He glances slowly around the clearing, and now, as his eyes meet ours, you grasp the depth of his hatred. But there is triumph there too —revengeful, triumphant hate. Suddenly, as though his face were not giving quite complete expression to his feelings, he throws his whole body into harmony with his mood. He swiftly snaps his hands on his hips, arches his shoulders, plants his feet wide apart. It is a magnificent gesture of defiance, of burning contempt for this place now and all that it has stood for in the twenty-two years since it witnessed the humbling of the German Empire.

*William L. Shirer, June 21, 1940* [24n]

## THE OCCUPATION OF NORWAY

• I attach this measure of importance to the occupation of Norway because I cannot understand, even in retrospect, how it was that the powerful British Navy did not succeed in defeating, or at least in hindering, an operation which did not have even the support of the very modest German naval forces. If the Norwegian

the war, threatening France on its southeastern border. France was finished. In 40 days, it had been crushed and beaten. Millions of her soldiers were prisoners; the rest were dispirited and defeated.

When he heard the news of France's downfall, Hitler performed a peculiar hopping dance step that seemed a ludicrous gesture for a conquering war hero. But he had kept his promise to the German people: the humiliation of 1918 had been obliterated. For the formal surrender, Hitler decreed that the signing take place in the old Wagon Lit in the Forest of Compiegne, where Marshal Foch had presented the 1918 armistice terms

campaign had failed, we should not have been able to create the conditions which were a pre-requisite for the success of our submarines. Without the coast of Norway at our disposal, we should not have been able to launch our attacks against the ports of the Midlands and Northern Britain, and operations in the Arctic waters would also have been impracticable.

*Hitler, April 24, 1942* [12j]

### THE BATTLE OF BRITAIN

• I believe that the end of this war will mark the beginning of a durable friendship with England. But first we must give her the k.o.—for only so can we live at peace with her, and the Englishman can only respect someone who has first knocked him out. . . .

. . . But I've met a lot of Englishmen and Englishwomen whom I respect. Let's not think too much about those whom we know, with whom we've had those deceptive official dealings—they're not men.

Despite everything, it's only with the people that we can associate.

*Hitler, July 22, 1941* [12k]

• First of all, a Nazi victory means a victory over Great Britain. As long as one important nation in Europe does not come to terms with Hitler and maintains a naval blockade of the European coast line, the Nazis cannot breathe; they cannot get access to the supplies or markets of the outside world. They must break through this ring of ships in order to have any real victory. The victory over Britain must be so complete that the British fleet is either destroyed, captured, or driven permanently away from its European bases. If this occurs, Britain is doomed.

*Douglas Miller, 1941* [19a]

• The Battle of Britain, the by now legendary air battle over England that began on August 13, 1940 ("Eagle Day"), with the first major raids on airfields and radar

to Germany. Under the terms of the surrender, France was divided into two parts. Occupied, or Vichy, France was headed by the aging Marshal Henri Pétain, who was to carry out increasingly humiliating German directives. The rest of France—"Free France"—would eventually also fall under German control.

In Norway, all resistance ended in June. Now only Britain remained, and Hitler expected the British to sue for peace shortly. To the Führer, the war was practically over. Hitler waited for more than a month for an overture. When none came, he launched the Luftwaffe in ferocious air attacks against the

stations in the south of England, had to be broken off on September 16 after heavy losses because of bad weather conditions. The Luftwaffe had failed to achieve any one of its goals. British industrial potential had not been struck a really heavy blow, nor had the populace been psychologically crushed, nor had the Luftwaffe won air superiority. And although Admiral Raeder had reported a few days before that the navy was ready for the landing operation, Hitler postponed the project "for the present."

*Joachim C. Fest, 1973* [6k]

• Now Goering made the first of his two tactical errors. The skill of British Fighter Command in committing its planes to battle against vastly superior attacking forces was based on its shrewd use of radar. From the moment they took off from their bases in Western Europe the German aircraft were spotted on British radar screens, and their course so accurately plotted that Fighter Command knew exactly where and when they could best be attacked. This was something new in warfare and it puzzled the Germans, who were far behind the British in the development and use of this electronic device. . . .

And then suddenly Goering made his second tactical error, this one comparable in its consequences to Hitler's calling off the armored attack on Dunkirk on May 24. It saved the battered, reeling R.A.F. and marked one of the major turning points of history's first great battle in the air.

With the British fighter defense suffering losses in the air and on the ground which it could not for long sustain, the Luftwaffe switched its attack on September 7 to massive night bombings of London. The R.A.F. fighters were reprieved.

*William L. Shirer, 1960* [240]

• A moral breakdown such as we experienced in November 1918 can be brought about in England only with great difficulty, if at all. We should have no illusions in this respect and should not place hopes in a type of warfare that was

Toward the end of World War II, Hitler would walk through the rubble of a destroyed German village (below left). But in the spring of 1940, he enjoyed nothing but victory. On June 21, he danced a jig of joy (below center) at Compiègne where, on November 11, 1918, Germany had surrendered to the Western powers. Now, in the same railway car (below right) where the World War I armistice was signed, France accepted a "harsh and merciless" treaty that divided her into two zones, one occupied by Germany, the other unoccupied. After leaving Compiègne, Hitler went to Paris with some of his aides (opposite page), including Albert Speer, who is on Hitler's right.

British cities in what the world viewed as a preliminary softening attack for an invasion (called Operation Sea Lion by Hitler and his associates).

Now, as master of half of Europe, he set about creating a system of government resembling the rigid structure he had imposed on Germany. Mostly, he failed. As Telford Taylor, a lawyer and prosecutor at the Nuremberg war crimes trial commented in a study of German victories: "German occupation policies were not only harsh and ultimately atrocious; they were haphazard, and never were systematically formulated with an eye to achieving a victorious peace. It is true that many

once successful in the case of the German people, but in all likelihood will never succeed with the English.

*Goebbels, January 26, 1942* [18b]

• In one of two night air raids of especial intensity on London last week, a German bomb crashed into the House of Commons, destroying it beyond repair. Others unroofed Westminster Hall and the British Museum, and one put the broadcasting apparatus of Big Ben out of commission but left the four faces of the old clock still telling the passage of time. On each of the raids thousands of incendiaries also were dropped.

Newsweek, *May 19, 1941, p. 24*

### OPERATION SEA LION

• It remains a possibility . . . that Hitler never seriously considered the landing in England but employed the project merely as a weapon in the war of nerves. From the autumn of 1939 on, the military authorities, especially the commander in chief of the navy, Admiral Raeder, had repeatedly but vainly tried to interest him in the problems of a landing operation. And, in fact, as soon as Hitler assented to the plan he began introducing reservations and mentioning difficulties of the sort he had never previously recognized. . . .

. . . Hitler's qualms were not connected solely with his complexes about England. Rather, he well understood the type of resistance Churchill had alluded to. A world power with remote overseas bases had all sorts of ways of holding out. Invasion or conquest of the motherland was not necessarily defeat. For example, England could go on fighting from Canada, could draw him deeper and deeper into the conflict in the wrong area, and finally involve him in the dreaded war with the United States.

*Joachim C. Fest, 1973* [61]

• . . . the mountainous secret German

London: A building hit by a German bomb tumbles to the ground.

others shared with Hitler the blame for these shortcomings. But on the loom of history, autocrats must meet the pragmatic test."

On September 27, 1940, Hitler concluded a three-power military and economic pact with Italy and Japan. Each nation promised full aid to any one attacked by an outsider. The ground was set for U.S. entry into the conflict. Hitler remained boundlessly optimistic. Germany, he said, "is strong enough to meet any combination in the world."

He saw Mussolini again in October, conferred with General Franco, and met with Marshal Pétain to reach an agreement on the principle of Franco-German collaboration. He also began

military files leave no doubt that Hitler's plan to invade Britain in the early fall of 1940 was deadly serious and that, though given to many hesitations, the Nazi dictator seriously intended to carry it out if there were any reasonable chance of success. Its ultimate fate was settled not by any lack of determination or effort but by the fortunes of war, which . . . began to turn against him.

*William L. Shirer, 1960* [24D]

I. Again and again I wrote these words-- the Abolition of the Treaty of Versailles. Not because it was a quixotic idea of my own, but because the Treaty of Versailles was the greatest injustice and the most infamous maltreatment of a great nation in recorded history and because it was impossible for our nation to continue to exist in the future unless Germany was free of this stranglehold.

*Hitler, January 30, 1941* [22dd]

## HITLER'S PROGRAM

## A TINY, UNSYMPATHETIC NEIGHBOR

• My program was to abolish the Treaty of Versailles. It is futile nonsense for the rest of the world to pretend today that I did not reveal this program until 1933, or 1935, or 1937. Instead of listening to the foolish chatter of émigrés, these gentlemen would have been wiser to read what I have written—and rewritten thousands of times. No human being has declared or recorded what he wanted more often than

• Never will the German people forget the attitude of the Swiss during this war. A nation of 80,000,000, while fighting for bare existence, finds itself almost uninterruptedly attacked, insulted, and slandered by the newspapers of a tiny State whose Government claims to be neutral.

*Frankfurter Zeitung,*
quoted in *The Times* (London),
December 10, 1940, page 5

to forge the Balkan treaties that were to align Hungary, Romania, and Bulgaria with the Axis, lead to the invasion of Yugoslavia the next April, and, finally, to bring a friendship pact with Britain's eastern ally, Turkey.

In the United States, President Franklin D. Roosevelt was clearly worried. "The Nazi masters of Germany intend to enslave the whole of Europe and then to use the resources of Europe to dominate the world," he declared. Hitler countered by declaring that German submarines would sink any ship that "comes before our torpedo tubes."

German troops had poured through Romania and Bulgaria

## PEOPLE OF THE OCCUPIED LANDS

• We can even learn a lesson from the way the French behaved in Alsace. Without the slightest regard for the generations of men who would have to suffer in consequence, they set to work to eradicate from Alsace every vestige and trace of German influence, thrusting brutally the customs and the culture of France down the throats of the inhabitants. Acting in the same way we will mercilessly wipe out bilingualism in these territories, and the radical methods to which we shall have recourse will themselves prove their efficiency, even on the population hostile to Germanisation. We shall rapidly achieve a clear-cut situation, so that, by the second generation, or at latest by the third, these regions will have been completely pacified.

As regards Alsace and Lorraine, if we want to re-make these into authentic German provinces, then we must drive out all those who do not voluntarily accept the fact that they are Germans.

*Hitler, at dinner, May 12, 1942* [121]

• I do not think, therefore, that we should sanction, except in isolated cases, marriage between our soldiers and foreign women. The request may often be based on sound reasons, but all the same it should be refused. Most of these cases, obviously, result from a sexual experience which the applicant desires to continue— and the number of requests submitted to me is enormous. It suffices, however, to glance at the photographs of most of the candidates to realise that in the majority of cases the union is not desirable. Most of the women concerned are either malformed or ugly, and from the racial point of view the results could not be satisfactory. I am sure, too, that such marriages would not stand the test of time.

*Hitler, April 24, 1942* [12m]

• There are a large number of Bulgarians who have studied engineering or taken their degrees in Germany. It would be a good policy to facilitate the taking of degress by foreigners at our universities, and we shall make friends for life of men who

Hitler marches beside a saluting Franco during the Führer's visit to Spain (October 23, 1940). Though Franco was indebted to Hitler and Mussolini for their help during the Spanish Civil War, he resisted joining them in World War II.

spent some of their youth in this fashion.

*Hitler, April 10, 1942* [12n]

• The brutal myth underlying Nazi racial doctrine was subsequently expanded to include the enslavement of the subjugated peoples, especially those of Eastern Europe. The counterpart to this was the idea of the "transnationalizing" (*"Umvolkung"*) of racially valuable elements, of the selection of blond, blue-eyed potential Germans from kindred peoples. In Germany, a racist population policy and "eugenics" were instituted, with measures ranging from barbaric sterilization to racially desirable breeding. Here, however, the regime did run up against some obstacles and even opposition, particularly from the churches.

*Karl Dietrich Bracher, 1969* [3b]

• Hitler's fine rhetoric about drawing labor out of a population of two hundred fifty million came to nought, partly because of the ineffectiveness of the German administration in the occupied territories, partly because of the preference of the men involved for taking to the forests and joining the partisans sooner than be dragged off for labor service in Germany.

*Albert Speer, 1969* [25d]

### HITLER AND MUSSOLINI

• Hitler's features were flabby; his forehead, his nose, and his mouth were mean, his expression set, dismal, and vulgar. His eyes, globular and dull gray, came to life only in anger or in a trance; he rolled his *r*s so that they rang like rocks in an avalanche. His gait was stiff; he rarely smiled or laughed.

Mussolini was molded with more art. His cast of features was after the pattern of Caesar's: a broad brow, his, a square jaw, an avid and greedy mouth. His face was mobile: in a flash it reflected the most contrary feelings. His swart complexion afforded a fine background for his jet-

by early March of 1941. The previous October, Mussolini had invaded Greece, but had not been able to make any progress. German panzers came to his aid in April, rolling through Yugoslavia and reaching Athens before the month's end. At the same time, Axis forces under Field Marshal Rommel drove the British forces in North Africa to the Egyptian border. In May, German parachute troops occupied Crete.

Success came from every side, but Hitler had already made his basic mistake. He had flinched from an invasion of Great Britain, a decision that historians still puzzle over. If he had conquered Britain, or at least lulled her into making peace, he

black, flashing eyes. His voice was sharp, his speech precipitous. His back arched, he stood before his audience, prompt, supple, and agile. His smile was subtle, his laughter truculent.

*André François-Poncet, 1946* [7d]


• If the Duce were to die, it would be a great misfortune for Italy. As I walked with him in the gardens of the Villa Borghese, I could easily compare his profile with that of the Roman busts, and I realised he was one of the Caesars. There's no doubt at all that Mussolini is the heir of the great men of that period.

*Hitler, July 21, 1941* [12o]


• I hold the Duce in the highest esteem, because I regard him as an incomparable statesman. On the ruins of a ravished Italy he has succeeded in building a new State which is a rallying point for the whole of his people.

*Hitler, April 23, 1942* [12p]

## URGING ON THE JAPANESE

• Hitler wanted Japan to enter the war at the earliest possible moment, but it was against England, not against Russia, that he sought her cooperation. The war in Europe, Hitler and Ribbentrop assured Matsuoka, was virtually over; it was only a question of time before Britain was forced to admit that she had been defeated. An attack by Japan upon Singapore would not only have a decisive effect in convincing Britain that there was no further point in continuing the war, it would also provide the key to the realization of Japanese ambitions in Eastern Asia at a time when circumstances formed a unique combination in her favour. 'There could never in human imagination,' Hitler told Matsuoka, 'be a better condiiton for a joint effort of the Tripartite Pact countries than the one which had now been produced. . . .'

. . . In all their conversations Hitler and Ribbentrop persistently urged on Matsuoka the importance of an attack on Singapore at the earliest possible date. 'Japan

would have had a free hand in remolding continental Europe to his liking.

Also in May—on the tenth—a journey occurred that electrified the world. Rudolf Hess, now a cabinet minister in Hitler's government, flew a Messerschmitt-110 to Scotland, where he parachuted out of the plane and, upon landing, asked a local farmer to take him to the home of the Duke of Hamilton, whom he had met in 1936. The next day, in a meeting with the Duke, Hess claimed "that the Führer . . . wished to stop the fighting." In the following days it became apparent that Hess was not an emissary from Hitler, but that the flight had been his own idea

would best help the common cause,' Ribbentrop declared, 'if she did not allow herself to be diverted by anything from the attack on Singapore,' and he asked the Japanese Foreign Minister for maps of the British base, 'so that the Führer, who must certainly be considered the greatest expert of modern times on military matters, could advise Japan as to the best method for the attack on Singapore.' Japan, in short, was to play in the Far East the role for which Hitler had cast Franco's Spain and Mussolini's Italy: the capture of Singapore was the Far Eastern version of the capture of Gibraltar and the drive on Suez.

*Alan Bullock, 1962* [40]

• Singapore has become a symbol to the entire world. Before 1914, it was only a commercial harbour. It was between the two wars that Singapore began its great rise and acquired the strategic importance that it's recognised to have to-day. When one builds a citadel like Singapore, it must be made an impregnable position—else it's a waste of money. The English have lived on the idea of an invincibility whose image is invoked for them by the magic names of Shanghai, Hongkong and Singapore. Suddenly they have to sing smaller, and realize that this magnificent façade was merely a bluff. I agree, it's a terrible blow for the English.

*Hitler, February 2, 1942* [12q]

### CONQUERED PEOPLE TO THE EAST

• Rumania would do well to give up, as far as possible, the idea of having her own industry. She would direct the wealth of her soil, and especially her wheat, towards the German market. She would receive from us, in exchange, the manufactured goods she needs. Bessarabia is a real granary. Thus the Rumanian proletariat, which is contaminated by Bolshevism, would disappear, and the country would never lack anything.

*Hitler, July 25, 1941* [12r]

and had occurred without any foreknowledge by Hitler and other Nazi leaders. Hitler, embarrassed by the affair, told the world that Hess had become insane, and stripped his former comrade of his position. Martin Bormann, who had been active in the Nazi party for a number of years, replaced Hess as deputy leader of the party.

As the uproar subsided, Hitler returned his attention to a plan that he had written about in *Mein Kampf* some 17 years earlier, and that now was well on its way toward being implemented: Operation Barbarossa, the invasion of the Soviet Union.

On June 22, 1941, in a move that surprised the world and

---

• Nothing would be a worse mistake on our part than to seek to educate the masses there. It is to our interest that the people should know just enough to recognise the signs on the roads. At present they can't read, and they ought to stay like that. But they must be allowed to live decently, of course, and that's also to our interest.

We'll take the southern part of the Ukraine, especially the Crimea, and make it an exclusively German colony. There'll be no harm in pushing out the population that's there now.

*Hitler, July 27, 1941* [12s]

• Personally, I believe we must change our policies essentially as regards the peoples of the East. We could reduce the danger of the Partisans considerably if we succeeded in at least winning a certain measure of confidence with these peoples. A clear peasant and church policy would work wonders there. It might also be useful to set up sham governments in the various sectors which would then have to be responsible for unpleasant and unpopu-

lar measures. Undoubtedly it would be easy to set up such sham governments, and we would then always have a façade behind which to camouflage our policies. I shall talk to the Fuehrer about this problem in the near future. I consider it one of the most vital in the present situation in the East.

*Goebbels, May 22, 1942* [18c]

### HESS FLIES TO SCOTLAND

• Hess's motives are clear. He sincerely wanted peace with Britain. He had not the shadow of a doubt that Germany would win the war and destroy the United Kingdom unless peace were concluded at once. There were, to be sure, other motives. The war had brought his personal eclipse. Running the Nazi Party as Hitler's deputy during the war was dull business and no longer very important. What mattered in Germany now was running the war and foreign affairs. These were the things which engaged the attention of the Fuehrer

Hitler addresses the Reichstag.

to the exclusion of almost all else, and which put the limelight on Goering, Ribbentrop, Himmler, Goebbels and the generals. Hess felt frustrated and jealous. How better restore his old position with his beloved Leader and in the country than by pulling off a brilliant and daring stroke of statesmanship such as singlehandedly arranging peace between Germany and Britain?

*William L. Shirer, 1960* [24q]

• The sensational prize capture was hushed by the British Government for two days. Actually, the first news of the disappearance of Hess came from Berlin. On May 12 Nazi party headuarters announced that Hess had taken off in a plane at Augsburg and that he had crashed or met with some other misfortune. As the Berlin radio announced that the Deputy Führer had committed suicide, Nazi officials prepared for all contingencies by declaring that Hess suffered from a mental derangement.

*Newsweek, May 19, 1941, p. 23*

• What bothered [Hitler] was that Churchill might use the incident to pretend to Germany's allies that Hitler was extending a peace feeler. "Who will believe me when I say that Hess did not fly there in my name, that the whole thing is not some sort of intrigue behind the backs of my allies?" Japan might even alter her policy because of this, he fretted. He put through a phone call to Ernest Udet, the famous First World War fighter pilot and now technical chief of the air force, and wanted to know whether the two-motored plane Hess was using could reach its goal in Scotland and what weather conditions it would encounter. After a brief interval Udet called back to say that Hess was bound to fail for navigational reasons alone; because of the prevailing side winds he would probably fly past England and into empty space. For a moment Hitler regained hope: "If only he would drown in the North Sea! Then he would vanish without a trace, and we could work out some harmless explanation at our leisure." But after a few hours his anxieties returned, and in order to anticipate the British in any case he decided to announce over the

apparently Josef Stalin himself, Germany marched across the Russian border. In less than a month, Hitler's armored divisions had smashed more than 300 miles inside Russia. Hitler thought that by September Russia, too, would be his. But German forces were now thinly stretched out along the 1,000 mile front from Finland to the Black Sea, and Russian resistance was stiffening.

Hitler's generals wanted to attack Moscow, but their commander-in-chief insisted on a great pincer movement against the Soviet army east of Kiev. Hitler wanted the rich Ukraine. By September, Hitler's crystal-ball month for victory, the German blitzkrieg had slowed down. Communications and supply lines

radio that Hess had gone mad. . . .

At the time it appeared to me that Bormann's ambition had driven Hess to this desperate act. Hess, also highly ambitious, could plainly see himself being excluded from access to and influence over Hitler. . . . Twenty-five years later, in Spandau prison, Hess assured me in all seriousness that the idea had been inspired in him in a dream by supernatural forces. He said he had not at all intended to oppose or embarrass Hitler. "We will guarantee England her empire; in return she will give us a free hand in Europe." That was the message he took to England—without managing to deliver it. It had also been one of Hitler's recurrent formulas before and occasionally even during the war.

*Albert Speer, 1969* [25e]

**THE INVASION OF RUSSIA**

• Today something like 160 Russian divisions are standing at our frontiers. For weeks constant violations of this frontier have taken place, not only affecting us but from the far North down to Rumania. Russian airmen consider it sport nonchalantly to overlook these frontiers, presumably to prove to us that they already feel themselves masters of these territories. During the night of June 17th to June 18th Russian patrols again penetrated into Reich territory and could only be driven back after prolonged firing. This has brought us to the hour when it is necessary for us to take steps against this plot devised by the Jewish Anglo-Saxon war mongers and equally the Jewish rulers of the Bolshevik center in Moscow.

*Hitler, June 22,1941* [22aa]

• In the morning of June 22nd, this greatest battle in world history began. Since then somewhat more than three and a half months have passed, and today I can make the following statement. Everything since then has proceeded according to plan. . . . We misjudged one thing, however. We had no conception of the

were too long and the terrain too difficult for fast movement.

German troops had not reached their objectives of Stalingrad, Moscow, and Leningrad, and the long, severe Russian winter was about to begin. The Battle for Stalingrad was to last six months and result in Germany's greatest defeat—the turning point of World War II.

gigantic preparations of this enemy against Germany and Europe, of how tremendously great this danger really was, and how very narrowly we escaped this time the annihilation not only of Germany but of all of Europe. Today I can reveal this. I say this for the first time today because now I can state that this enemy has been defeated and will never rise again.

*Hitler, October 3, 1941* [22bb]

• There is evidence to show that when the German armies entered the Ukraine and the Baltic States they were looked upon as liberators. The treatment the local population received from the civil administration and the S.S. who moved in behind the armies rapidly destroyed these illusions. Ignoring all that might have been done to drive a wedge between the people and the Soviet Government, especially in the Ukraine, Hitler preferred to treat the inhabitants of Eastern Europe indiscriminately as Slav *Untermenschen,* fit only for slave labour.

*Alan Bullock, 1962* [4D]

• [Hitler] made a brief pause, then in an icy tone continued: "If the war is lost, the people will be lost also. It is not necessary to worry about what the German people will need for elemental survival. On the contrary, it is best for us to destroy even these things. For the nation has proved to be the weaker, and the future belongs solely to the stronger eastern nation. In any case only those who are inferior will remain after this struggle, for the good have already been killed."

*Albert Speer, 1969* [25f]

# 8

# THE END

Already commander-in-chief of the armed forces, Hitler now took on the specific title of commander of the Wehrmacht. He had aged, worn out more by nervous stress than by his years. He was living almost permanently at his general staff headquarters at Rastenburg (the Wolf's Lair) in East Prussia or at Vinnitsa in the Ukraine. He made fewer and fewer trips to Berlin, Munich, and Berchtesgaden, his beloved mountain retreat in Bavaria.

The Russians launched their first major offensive on December 6, 1941. It was the first serious military threat to the Third Reich. The next day the Japanese attacked Pearl Harbor and other U.S. bases in the Pacific. The United States was in the war. Hitler did not wait for the United States; he declared war first. The news stunned the German people, who were already weary of the war. Here was a huge new enemy with vast military and economic potential. They remembered that America had been the ultimate factor in bringing about the downfall of Germany in the first World War.

Hitler and his Nazi advisers loudly proclaimed their faith in German arms and boasted of victory. However, Hitler admitted that Germany was now on the defensive. In his New Year's message, he warned the German people of the hard fighting

144

"Exemplary Pupils of the Berlin Governess"—Soviet depiction of the relationship between Germany, Italy, and Japan.

The Russian winter: Mud traps men, machines, and armored cars, greatly slowing the German advance toward Moscow.

ahead and declared that Russia would be beaten in 1942. "God Almighty will assist us in the coming year," he said.

With the arrival of winter, the improperly clad German troops could not withstand Russia's blizzards and paralyzing cold. At Stalingrad, in Feburary, 1942, 330,000 soldiers of the German Sixth Army were killed and a German field marshal and his staff were captured. Hitler blamed the weather—it was Russia's severest winter in 140 years—and vowed he would take the city in the summer. Troops were needed to replace those lost in the fighting. Mussolini promised to send additional Italian troops to the Russian front and recruiting in Hungary and Ro-

## AN OPINION OF NAZISM

• What does Nazi Germany stand for? First, for the principle of force instead of law. The Nazis have so little respect for written law that they have not even bothered to abolish the previous Weimar Constitution. . . .

. . . Nazism, as I see it, meant that the German people became tired of beggary and turned to crime on a world scale. Some of us still remember the Ten Commandments we used to learn in Sunday School. As I run them over in my mind, it seems that the Nazis flagrantly violate all ten of them as a matter of common practice.

*Douglas Miller, 1941* [19b]

## THE U.S. ENTERS THE WAR

• There was a basic contradiction from the beginning in Hitler's policy toward America. Though he had only contempt for her military prowess he endeavored during the first two years of the conflict to keep her out of the war. This, as we have seen, was the main task of the German Embassy in Washington, which went to great lengths, including the bribing of Congressmen, attempting to subsidize writers and aiding the America First Committee, to support the American isolationists and thus help to keep America from joining Germany's enemies in the war.

*William L. Shirer, 1960* [24r]

• Germany and Italy went to war with the United States last week in the most leisurely and formal manner in which they have entered a conflict with any nation so far. For four days after the attack on Pearl Harbor nothing happened. Then on Dec. 11 both Hitler and Mussolini summoned the human sounding boards they use when important declarations are made. The Führer convened the Reichstag and the Duce called thousands of Black Shirts to

mania was surprisingly successful.

Meantime, German industry was pressed in an all-out effort to maximize production. The industrial and human resources of the occupied territories were exploited with even greater brutality. Mass deportations of foreign laborers to the factories of the Reich were intensified. Prisoners of war were also put to work in armament factories and elsewhere. Though this was in violation of the Hague and Geneva conventions, these prisoners, if they managed to survive, were comparatively fortunate— many prisoners were left to die from starvation, exposure, and disease. Two million Russian soldiers died as German prisoners

the Piazza Venezia.

Hitler's speech was a hoarse challenge to the United States in which the Führer's voice sometimes rose almost to the point of hysteria. But there was a curious lack of the usual ominous threats and trumpetings of imminent victory.

Newsweek, *December 22, 1941, p. 37*

way, even the drumming of our own planes patrolling the threatened city— none of these sounds was particularly reassuring. We weren't exactly afraid, but unlike one nerveless hero we met, we weren't exactly bored, either.

The New Yorker, *December 20, 1941, p. 9*

● Any attempt to tell how people felt in New York during the first days of war necessarily has a personal basis. Our own emotions covered quite a good deal of ground. We wish we could say that we looked forward to being bombed with the calm fatalism recommended by our London friends, but we didn't. Logic (and the military experts) told us there was no appreciable danger, but the peril was too far outside our experience—something that might come in from the sea without warning, very high and nearly silent, as impersonal as lightning. The wail of the sirens coming up thinly from the street, the controlled voice on the radio telling of destruction already conceivably on its

## RUSSIAN INVASION STALLED

● Even this year the winter wouldn't have caused us any difficulties if it hadn't surprised us by its suddenness. Yet it's lucky it came so suddenly, for otherwise we'd have advanced another two or three hundred kilometres. In that case, the adaptation of the railway to our gauge wouldn't have been possible. In such temperatures, we're obliged to have recourse to traction by animals.

*Hitler, January 12, 1942* [12u]

of war; another million have never been accounted for. Western prisoners were treated less harshly, though many captured flyers were murdered.

Hitler urged Himmler to push forward with the "new order" in Europe, which meant the annihilation of the Jews and other races the Nazis considered impure. New concentration camps were built and older ones expanded. A new twist in Nazi horror tactics was introduced: extermination camps such as Auschwitz, Buchenwald, and Dachau, and mobile extermination squads that roamed Europe. Indeed, as Germany's position deteriorated, as her physical resources became more depleted, the

• We are receiving reports about the extraordinarily low morale of the Bolshevik troops along the border of Manchukuo. But I prevent publication of such information because it might awaken too great hopes in the German people. I am very keen about holding such reports back. The German people must face the hard facts of war and must not nurture empty hopes.

*Goebbels, January 21, 1942* [18d]

• In February and March, 1942, letters began to arrive again from my friends on the Leningrad front; they were in a critical situation as a result of vigorous and successful Russian thrusts.

*Gerhard Boldt, 1947* [2a]

• Had it not been for the mud and rain last October, we should have been in Moscow in no time. We have now learnt that the moment the rain comes, we must stop everything.

*Hitler, August 9, 1942* [12v]

## THE SIEGE AT STALINGRAD

• The concentration of effort in the defence of Stalingrad is a grave mistake on the part of the Russians. The victor in war is he who commits the fewest number of mistakes, and who has, also, a blind faith in victory. If the Russians had not decided to make a stand at Stalingrad, they would have done so elsewhere; but it does prove that a name can give a place significance which bears no relation to its intrinsic value.

*Hitler, September 6, 1942* [12w]

• There are reports . . . that [Germans] are again listening to foreign radio stations. The reason for this, of course, is our completely obscure news policy of no longer giving the people any insight into the war situation. Also, our reticence regarding Stalingrad and the fate of our missing soldiers there naturally leads the families to listen to Bolshevik radio stations, as these always broadcast the names

campaign against the Jews grew in intensity and effectiveness. Among his reasons for hating the Jews was Hitler's belief that they were responsible for Germany's losses. On October 25, 1941, he said: "From the rostrum of the Reichstag I prophesied to Jewry that, in the event of war's proving inevitable, the Jew would disappear from Europe. That race of criminals has on its conscience the two million dead of the first World War, and now already hundreds of thousands more. . . . It's not a bad idea, by the way, that public rumour attributes to us a plan to exterminate the Jews. Terror is a salutary thing." [12aa]

The chief victims were the Jews of Germany, Poland, and the

Buchenwald: Piles of emaciated bodies were found by horrified Allied soldiers (April 1945).

Soviet Union. By the war's end, Hitler's "final solution" to what he termed the Jewish problem had taken an estimated six million lives. When Allied armies penetrated Germany and rolled east, discovering one torture camp after another, they were literally sickened. Evidence was uncovered that hordes of Jewish captives had been scientifically murdered. Others were mutilated and made the subjects of ghoulish medical experiments. In addition, hundreds of thousands had died of disease, starvation, and maltreatment. When the world learned of the human depravity of the Nazi regime, the reaction was wholesale revulsion. Whatever stains were left on Germany by

---

of German soldiers reported as prisoners.
*Goebbels, May 25, 1943* [18e]

**THE RUSSIANS TURN THE TIDE**

● Stalingrad had shaken us—not only the tragedy of the Sixth Army's soldiers, but even more, perhaps, the question of how such a disaster could have taken place under Hitler's orders. For hitherto there had always been a success to offset every setback; hitherto there had been a new triumph to compensate for all losses or at least make everyone forget them. Now for the first time we had suffered a defeat for which there was no compensation. . . .

. . . At the beginning of the war in the east, Hitler, captive to his theory that the Slavs were subhuman, had called the war against them child's play. But the longer the war lasted, the more the Russians gained his respect. He was impressed by the stoicism with which they had accepted their early defeats. He spoke admiringly of Stalin, particularly stressing the parallels to his own endurance.
*Albert Speer, 1969* [25g]

● The situation in the East is engaging public attention far beyond any other topic. Moscow claims our retreat was not orderly but developed into a wild rout. That is not in accordance with the facts, but it is true that we have had to abandon tremendous quantities of supplies which we could neither take along nor destroy; and of course it is impossible to dynamite all military installations. Their advance is giving the Bolsheviks tremendous material advantages which will cause us grave difficulties.
*Goebbels, September 25, 1943* [18f]

● Invariably, Hitler ordered the bends in the front to be held at all costs, and just as invariably the Soviet forces would overrun the position after a few days or weeks. Then there followed new rages, mingled with fresh denunciations of the officers and, frequently, complaints against the German soldiers: "The soldier of the

August 25, 1944: American troops enter Paris, ending four years of occupation by the Germans.

First World War was much tougher. Think of all they had to go through, in Verdun, on the Somme. Today, they would run away from that kind of thing". . . .

. . . Even when the troops were retreating, he would declare triumphantly: "Didn't I order so and so three days ago? Again my order hasn't been carried out. They' don't carry out my orders and afterward they lie and blame the Russians. They lie when they say the Russians prevented them from carrying out the order." Hitler refused to admit that his failures were due to the weak position into which he had cast us by insisting on a war on many fronts.

*Albert Speer, 1969* [25h]

## WARTIME PROPAGANDA

• Propaganda destined for abroad must not in any way be based on that used for home consumption.

Broadcasts to Britain, for example, must contain plenty of music of the kind that is popular among Britons. In this way, when their own transmitting stations starve them of music, they will acquire the habit of listening-in more and more to the concerts we broadcast for them. As regards news-bulletins to Britain, we should confine ourselves to plain statements of facts, without comment on their value or importance. News about British high finance, its interests in certain sections of the armament industry, in the leadership and conduct of the war should be given without comment, but couched in such a way that the British listeners will themselves draw their own conclusions. As the old saying has it, little drops of water will gradually wear the stone away.

For our own people we must broadcast not only the facts but also copious and precise commentaries on their importance and significance. Good propaganda must be stimulating. Our stations must therefore go on talking about the drunkard Churchill and the criminal Roosevelt on every possible occasion.

*Hitler, April 10, 1942* [12x]

the Nazis, none was more damning than their bestial treatment of the Jews.

In 1942, the tide of war turned against Germany. Rommel's forces were decisively defeated by the British in the crucial battle of El Alamein, in Egypt. Allied air squadrons appeared in German skies and began hammering away at cities and industrial installations. Even the fortunes of the U-boats were running out as the Allies intensified their anti-submarine warfare.

One of the biggest surprises to Hitler came in November of 1942, when an American army landed in North Africa. The

### A RELIGIOUS FIGURE

● I'm going to become a religious figure. Soon I'll be the great chief of the Tartars. Already Arabs and Moroccans are mingling my name with their prayers. Amongst the Tartars I shall become Khan. The only thing of which I shall be incapable is to share the sheiks' mutton with them. I'm a vegetarian, and they must spare me from their meat.

*Hitler, January 12, 1942* [12z]

### SENTENCING RESISTERS

● But above all, the war meant expansion; masses of new concentration-camp inmates poured in from the occupied territories. Hitler's infamous "Under Cover of Night" *("Nacht-und-Nebel")* decree of September, 1941, . . . ordered that anyone suspected of resistance be brought to Germany; after having served their sentences or being acquitted by special courts, such suspects were, on the basis of further decrees, to be handed over to the Gestapo. By this method, about 7,000 prisoners, mostly from France, were sent to concentration camps either directly or via prisons. Another group of camp inmates were Soviet prisoners of war, for whom special sections were set up in the camps; there the vast majority died of starvation.

*Karl Dietrich Bracher, 1969* [3c]

### THE JEWS WILL BE DESTROYED

● The end of the war will see the final ruin of the Jew. The Jew is the incarnation of egoism. And their egoism goes so far that they're not even capable of risking their lives for the defence of their most vital interests. . . .

. . . If the Jew weren't kept presentable by the Aryan, he'd be so dirty he couldn't open his eyes. We can live without the Jews, but they couldn't live without us.

Americans stormed city after city. Meantime, Rommel was being chased across the desert into Tunisia. Hitler ordered the occupation of Tunisia, and Axis troops seized the country before Allied troops got there. Hitler also sent troops into unoccupied France. To prevent the Germans from taking command of the French naval fleet, which was based at Toulon, French sailors sank the ships. On November 9, during the annual commemoration of the 1923 putsch, Hitler told his audience that the Allies were facing a Germany that would fight to the end. "In me," he declared "they . . . are facing an opponent who does not even think of the word capitulate."

When the Europeans realise that, they'll all become simultaneously aware of the solidarity that binds them together. The Jew prevents this solidarity. He owes his livelihood to the fact that this solidarity does not exist.

*Hitler, November 5, 1941* [12bb]

• We realize that this war can only end in the wiping out of the Germanic nations, or by the disappearance of Jewry from Europe. On September 3rd, I spoke in the Reichstag—and I dislike premature prophecies—and I said that this war would not end the way the Jews imagine, that is, in the extinction of the European Aryan nations, but that the result of this war would be the destruction of Jewry.

*Hitler, January 30, 1942* [22g]

## MASS SHOOTING OF JEWS IN THE UKRAINE

• The people who had got off the trucks, men, women and children of every age, had to undress on orders from an SS man who held a riding whip or dog whip in his hand. They had to deposit their clothing, shoes, upper and underclothes separately, at certain places. I saw a heap of shoes containing at a guess eight hundred to a thousand shoes, and huge piles of underclothing and clothing. Without an outcry or weeping these people undressed, stood together in family groups, kissed and said goodbye to each other, and waited for the beckoning gesture of another SS man who stood at the pit and likewise held a whip in his hand. . . . The completely naked people walked down a flight of steps that had been cut into the earthen wall of the pit, stumbled over the heads of those who were already lying there, to the place that the SS man indicated. They lay down in front of the dead or wounded; some stroked those who were still living and murmured what seemed to be words of comfort. Then I heard a series of shots. I looked into the pit and saw the bodies twitching, or the heads already lying still on the bodies in

By May, 1943, the Allies had forced the Germans and Italians to surrender Africa. In the last week of the campaign, some 240,000 Axis troops—the remnants of the Afrika Korps—surrendered to the Allies. For Hitler, it was another Stalingrad.

From Africa, Anglo-American forces invaded Sicily and then moved up the boot of Italy. Mussolini pleaded with Hitler for military aid, but Hitler advised his old friend to fall back to the River Po for a stand. Military targets near Rome were heavily bombarded by American planes, and the Italian people were in a panic. In July, Mussolini was ousted and arrested by the Fascists who, two months later in September, signed an arm-

front. Blood ran from the back of their necks.

*Herman Friedrich Gräbe,*
*at the Nuremberg trials* [28a]

## THE CONCENTRATION CAMPS

• We had two S.S. doctors on duty at Auschwitz to examine the incoming transports of prisoners. These would be marched by one of the doctors, who would make spot decisions as they walked by. Those who were fit to work were sent into the camp. Others were sent immediately to the extermination plants. Children of tender years were invariably exterminated since by reason of their youth they were unable to work.

Still another improvement we made over Treblinka was that at Treblinka the victims almost always knew that they were to be exterminated, while at Auschwitz we endeavored to fool the victims into thinking that they were to go through a delousing process. Of course, frequently they realized our true intentions and we sometimes had riots and difficulties. Very frequently women would hide their children under the clothes but of course when we found them we would send the children in to be exterminated.

We were required to carry out these exterminations in secrecy, but of course the foul and nauseating stench from the continuous burning of bodies permeated the entire area and all of the people living in the surrounding communities knew that exterminations were going on at Auschwitz.

*Rudolf Franz Hoess*
*(a commander at Auschwitz), 1946* [21b]

• "I read all about the myth of the six million and it's a known fact six million Jews could not have been killed by the Nazis. That wasn't their philosophy. People seem to believe their philosophy was genocide, but it wasn't."

*Sandra Silva (member,*
*American Nazi Party)*
*quoted in* The New York Times,
*June 6, 1974*

istice with the Allies. Hitler sent in German troops under Field Marshal Albert von Kesselring when an Anglo-American force landed in Salerno in mid-Italy. Kesselring was able to neutralize the Italian army and block the Allied advance north of Naples. On September 13, Mussolini was rescued from his mountain-top prison by German glider troops. After meeting with Hitler, who prodded him into proclaiming a new Italian Social Republic, Mussolini went to live in northern Italy, which was still under Axis control. His mistress joined him there. On April 26, 1945, while attempting to escape into Switzerland, both were caught by partisans and killed. Their bodies were taken to

Hitler and other officers examine a map of Germany.

Milan, where they were hung upside down from lampposts.

Throughout the summer of 1943, the German army managed to contain enemy operations on all fronts. Then, in the fall, Soviet troops massed a tremendous offensive that was to bring them to the borders of Bulgaria and Romania. British and American planes were systematically ruining Germany's industrial cities. The destruction was so widespread that, in effect, a "second front" had been established by the Allies. Cologne was paralyzed by the bombing. Punishing raids pounded the Ruhr Valley and the Krupp munitions complex in Essen. Hamburg, Germany's second largest city, was subjected to daily bombing

• To the Central Construction Office of the S.S. and Police, Auschwitz:

Subject: Crematoria 2 and 3 for the camp.

We acknowledge receipt of your order for five triple furnaces, including two electric elevators for raising the corpses and one emergency elevator. A practical installation for stoking coal was also ordered and one for transporting ashes.

*I. A. Topf & Sons, February 12, 1943* [28b]

• There is a core of some 120,000 regular readers of the *National Zeitung,* which for two decades has been whitewashing the Nazi era, "proving" that the only concentration and extermination camps were those built *after* the war by German prisoners under American orders, for propaganda purposes (there are even pictures); promoting a brisk trade in Nazi medals, uniforms, weapons and other memorabilia, as well as books and recordings of speeches, party congresses, narrations of military campaigns (victorious ones), and

engaging in a fairly subtle anti-Semitism. There is no need for blatancy; after all the Jews were only the first and most conspicuous of Nazi targets. Twelve or so million non-Jews murdered by the Germans died just as painfully—facts that are almost daily branded as "lies" in letters to newspapers, occasionally in demonstrations, less infrequently in swastika-daubings and cemetery vandalism.

*Charles Lam Markmann,*
in The New Republic, *June 8, 1974, p. 17*

**THE ALLIES BOMB THE REICH**

• The Americans undertook a great daylight raid on Bremen and inflicted heavy industrial losses. It really gets your goat to think that the Anglo-Saxon air powers are now in a position to blast the Reich with such formidable day raids. We shall have to make a big effort to regain at least half of the lost ground.

*Goebbels, March 20, 1943* [18g]

and battered almost out of existence. In the Atlantic, German submarines had been all but cleared out by Allied warships.

In a New Year's message for 1944, Hitler admitted that the previous year "brought us our heaviest reverses." He sought to bolster morale by pointing out that the war had added to, rather than subtracted from, the Reich's territory. "National fanaticism" would win in the end, he asserted, despite many "difficult situations."

Words could not halt the Allied onslaught. The ramparts of Germany's "fortress Europe" were crumbling. Hitler sought to overcome dissatisfaction on the home front by threats of punish-

• The result of English air raids are gradually becoming evident. Our textile industry has been pretty badly hit. We are not in a position to meet our obligations about the Reich textile coupon card, that is, we can't call up the unused points. Whatever we still have in the way of reserves must be pumped into the distressed areas.

The letters addressed to me give me some worry. There's an unusual amount of criticism contained in them. . . . Above all, these letters keep asking why the Fuehrer does not visit the distressed air areas, why Goering isn't to be seen anywhere, and especially why the Fuehrer doesn't for once talk to the German people to explain the present situation.

*Goebbels, July 25, 1943* [18h]

## A NOTE OF ANXIETY?

• The Führer was slow to recognize, and even slower to admit, the importance of the operations now begun. On 8 November, after the break-through at El Alamein and on the actual day of the Allied landings in North-west Africa, he appeared in Munich for the customary celebration of the 1923 putsch. Drawing the familiar contrast between the Imperial Germany of 1918 and the Third Reich, he declared:

He who was then the Kaiser was a man lacking the strength to resist his enemies. But in me they have found an adversary who does not even think of the word 'capitulation'. Ever since I was a boy it has always been my habit—originally perhaps a bad one, but in the final resort a virtue—to have the last word. All our enemies may rest assured that while the Germany of that time (1918) laid down its arms at a quarter to twelve, I on principle have never finished before five minutes past twelve.

None the less, despite his confident tone, it was noticeable that Hitler was already arguing on the defensive, and at the end of his speech he went out of his way to answer those who criticized him for not speaking more frequently. Underneath the boasting and the sarcasm a note of anxiety was clearly to be detected.

*Alan Bullock, 1962* [4q]

ment and promises of victory if the people would endure the hardships and sacrifices. "Whatever sacrifices we have to bear now," he declared, "are not to be compared with what we would have to bear if we lost the war."

On July 20, 1944, Hitler attended a regular military briefing at the Wolf's Lair. In the middle of the meeting, a bomb exploded. Hitler escaped with minor injuries, although one arm appeared to be injured. He rushed to a radio to assure the German people "that I am unhurt and well, and secondly, that you should know of a crime unparalleled in German history. A very small clique of ambitious, irresponsible and, at the same

## LIVES VERSUS HITLER'S PRESTIGE

• Totally oblivious of his own responsibility for what had happened, the Führer spared no thought for the men he had driven to death or captivity. He could think only of the commanders who had capitulated: such ingratitude and disloyalty, he declared, were beyond his comprehension.

"The man should have shot himself just as the old commanders who threw themselves on their swords when they saw their cause was lost. That goes without saying. Even Varus gave his slave the order: 'Now kill me!' . . .

"What hurts me most, personally, is that I promoted him to Field-Marshal. I wanted to give him this final satisfaction. That's the last Field-Marshal I shall appoint in this war. You mustn't count your chickens before they are hatched. I don't understand that at all. So many people have to die, and then a man like that besmirches the heroism of so many others at the last minute. He could have freed him-

self from all sorrow and ascended into eternity and national immortality, but he prefers to go to Moscow. What kind of choice is that? It just doesn't make sense."

It was the comment of a supreme egotist, the complaint of a man who was to see in the sufferings and defeat of a nation only his own betrayal by a people unworthy of their Führer.

*Alan Bullock, 1962* [48]

## CAPITULATION IS IMPOSSIBLE

• Towards the end of January 1943 Paulus reported that the suffering of the troops, through cold, hunger, and epidemics, was no longer bearable, and that to continue fighting in such conditions was beyond human strength. Hitler was unmoved. For answer he sent Paulus the message:

Capitulation is impossible. The 6th Army will do its historic duty at Stalingrad until the last man, in order to make possible the reconstruction of the Eastern Front.

time, senseless and stupid officers had concocted a plot to eliminate me and, with me, the staff of the High Command of the Wehrmacht." [248]

Actually, many of Hitler's top generals had been involved, including Rommel and General Klaus von Stauffenberg, a military hero and the one who planted the bomb. The generals were convinced that Germany had lost the war and knew Hitler would not surrender. Every plotter was quickly hunted down, tried, and executed. "This time," said Hitler, "we shall settle accounts with them in the manner to which we National Socialists are accustomed." Rommel, the "desert fox," was forced to

Hitler did not hesitate to stoop to bribes: at the last moment he promoted Paulus to the rank of Field-Marshal in order to buy the loyalty of the commander whose troops he had deliberately condemned to death. 'There is no record in military history,' he remarked to Jodl, 'of a German Field-Marshal being taken prisoner.'

*Alan Bullock, 1962* [4r]

### IN A POW LABOR CAMP

• In a lonely valley in the Harz Mountains a widely ramified system of caves had been established before the war for the storage of vital military chemicals. Here, on December 10, 1943, I inspected the extensive underground installations where the V-2 was to be produced. In enormous long halls prisoners were busy setting up machinery and shifting plumbing. Expressionlessly, they looked right through me, mechanically removing their prisoners' caps of blue twill until our group had passed them.

I cannot forget a professor of the Pasteur Institute in Paris who testified as a witness at the Nuremberg Trial. He too was in the Central Works which I inspected that day. Objectively, without any dramatics, he explained the inhuman conditions in this inhuman factory. The memory is especially painful, the more so because he made his charge without hatred, sadly and brokenly and also astonished at so much human degeneracy.

The conditions for these prisoners were in fact barbarous, and a sense of profound involvement and personal guilt seizes me whenever I think of them. As I learned from the overseers after the inspection was over, the sanitary conditions were inadequate, disease rampant; the prisoners were quartered right there in the damp caves, and as a result the mortality among them was extraordinarily high.

*Albert Speer, 1969* [251]

### A BELIEF IN VICTORY

• . . . he made himself believe in his ultimate victory. In a sense he was wor-

swallow poison; after his death, Hitler ordered a state funeral, and sent a telegram to the widow: "Accept my sincerest sympathy for the heavy loss you have suffered with the death of your husband. The name of Field Marshal Rommel will be forever linked with the heroic battles in North Africa."

After the attempted assassination, Hitler's health deteriorated markedly. Frequently he had to remain in bed, weakened by intense stomach cramps and throat trouble. Migraine headaches racked him, and his arms and legs trembled convulsively. Doctors, trying to alleviate the symptoms, filled him with drugs.

The month before, on June 6, 1944, a huge Allied force made

shiping himself. He was forever holding up to himself a mirror in which he saw not only himself but also the confirmation of his mission by divine Providence. His religion was based on the "lucky break" which must necessarily come his way; his method was to reinforce himself by autosuggestion. The more events drove him into a corner, the more obstinately he opposed to them his certainty about the intentions of Fate. Naturally, he also soberly understood the military facts. But he transmuted them by his own faith and regarded even defeat as a secret guarantee, offered by Providence, of the coming victory. Sometimes he could realize the hopelessness of a situation, but he could not be shaken in his expectation that at the last moment Fate would suddenly turn the tide in his favor.

*Albert Speer, 1969* [25j]

### THE GENERAL'S PLOT

• The circle of these usurpers is very small and has nothing in common with the spirit of the German Wehrmacht and,

above all, none with the German people. It is a gang of criminal elements which will be destroyed without mercy.

I therefore give orders now that no military authority . . . is to obey orders from this crew of usurpers. I also order that it is everyone's duty to arrest, or, if they resist, to shoot at sight, anyone issuing or handling such orders. . . .

*Hitler, July 21, 1944* [24s]

• When [Wilhelm Keitel] picked himself up out of the dust immediately after the explosion and saw Hitler standing there relatively uninjured, he had rushed at him, as Hitler now repeatedly related, exclaiming: "*Mein Führer*, you're alive, you're alive!" and ignoring all convention had wildly embraced him. It was clear that after that Hitler would never drop him—he was even more closely than ever attached to him since Keitel seemed the right person to take harsh vengeance upon the rebels. "Keitel was almost killed himself," Hitler declared. "He will show no mercy."

*Albert Speer, 1969* [25k]

a successful landing in Normandy, France, and with D-Day began an almost uninterrupted swoop across Europe into the heart of Germany. Desperate and with his weakened armies falling back on all fronts, Hitler proclaimed on August 31 the total mobilization of all male citizens from ages 15 to 60. "In this war of destiny for the German people, everyone must fight and work for final victory. However long this war lasts, we shall never capitulate. We shall not give in at the eleventh hour. We shall go on fighting past 12 o'clock."

In the days just before Christmas, 1944, in a last, mighty effort to throw the Allied army back, the German panzers caught the

• After the General's Plot of 20th July [Hitler] had withdrawn from publicity,—withdrawn, or been withdrawn, so effectively that many believed him dead, or imprisoned by the all-powerful Himmler. As nothing but silence answered these suggestions, rumour and exaggeration quickly extended their scope, and supplied the circumstantial detail which so often passes for evidence.

*H. R. Trevor-Roper, 1947* [27a]

### THE NORMANDY INVASION

• This day [June 6, 1944] so crucial for the course of the war had not, as might have been expected, been at all a turbulent one. Especially in dramatic situations, Hitler tried to maintain his calm—and his staff imitated this self-control. It would have been an infraction of the usual tone of casual discourse to show nervousness or anxiety.

But during the following days and weeks, in characteristic but more and more absurd mistrust, Hitler remained convinced that the invasion was merely a feint whose purpose was to trick him into deploying his defensive forces wrongly. He continued to hold that the real invasion would take place at another spot which would have meanwhile been stripped of troops. The navy, too, considered the terrain unfavorable for large-scale landings, he declared. For the time being he expected the decisive assault to take place in the vicinity of Calais—as though he were determined that the enemy, too, would prove him to have been right. For there, around Calais, he had ever since 1942 been emplacing the heaviest naval guns under many feet of concrete to destroy an enemy landing fleet. This was the reason he did not commit the Fifteenth Army, stationed at Calais, to the battlefield on the coast of Normandy.

*Albert Speer, 1969* [251]

American army by surprise with a heavy attack near Bastogne, Belgium. Bad weather kept American air strength grounded and the Americans reeled back. But they held in two weeks of costly fighting and moved to the offensive. For Hitler and Germany, the Battle of the Bulge was the last hurrah.

At times, even Hitler seemed to realize that the war was lost. He was not rational at times. went into tirades, issued impossible orders. He vowed the whole of Germany would perish with him. On March 19, 1945, he ordered that the enemy was to find only "scorched earth" in their path into Germany. He spent his final days inside the air-raid bunker of the German Chancellory

• For months . . . the battle being waged there had proved exhausting for German fighting potential and had forced us to direct all available forces to that theater, particularly the elite of our Panzer divisions. Stalin's constant demands for a second front in France had ensured that the German High Command could not withdraw enough troops to push the Russians back across the Vistula and use the river as the backbone of a really strong line of defense.

*Gerhard Boldt, 1947* [2b]

## STREAMS OF REFUGEES

• By this time [March, 1945] the terrible, endless stream of despairing refugees from the east had grown to a torrent. On both sides of the major roads from the east there had arisen a wall of broken-down vehicles, of people and animals starved or frozen to death. Train after train rolled into the stations in Berlin with refugees from the east, many of whom had been snowed under in open cattle wagons and had died of frostbite. Everywhere there was unspeakable misery and distress.

But Adolf Hitler saw none of this, or did not *want* to see it, for fear of impairing his "inspiration". . . . for Hitler the war consisted only of figures, of blue and red lines on the General Staff maps. He never once arranged to be shown films of the actual destruction caused by bombing, which might have given him at least a vague picture of the reality. . . .

. . . Hitler had once called Churchill a "military idiot," but while Churchill was clambering over the rubble of London and inspiring the people with fresh courage, even visiting his soldiers just behind the front lines, smoking his cigar and armed with a walking stick, Adolf Hitler crawled off to hide in the forests of East Prussia behind barricades of heavily armed sentries and did not appear at the front or among the civilian population in the bomb-ravaged cities.

*Gerhard Boldt, 1947* [2c]

in Berlin. With him were Eva Braun, who had been his mistress for more than twelve years, Goebbels and his family, and most of the personal staff that had served during the Führer's dictatorship. By April, Russian troops were on the outskirts of Berlin. April 20 was Hitler's 56th birthday. The Nazi leaders gathered around him to give him their best wishes. They were all there for the last time.

The next day, Russian artillery fire could be heard in the heart of the city. Hitler ordered a counter-attack, which was impossible to mount. In the middle of the daily conference with his generals, the Führer exploded in a series of accusations

## HOROSCOPES PREDICT PEACE

• . . . in the course of the discussion [Goebbels and Hitler] sent for two horoscopes that were carefully kept in one of Himmler's research departments: the horoscope of the Fuehrer, drawn up on 30th January 1933, and the horoscope of the Republic, dated 9th September 1918. These sacred documents were fetched and examined, and "an astonishing fact" was discovered, which might well have repaid an earlier scrutiny. "Both horoscopes had unanimously predicted the outbreak of war in 1939, the victories till 1941, and then the series of defeats culminating in the worst disasters in the early months of 1945, especially the first half of April. Then there was to be an overwhelming victory for us in the second half of April, stagnation till August, and in August peace. After the peace there would be a difficult time for Germany for three years; but from 1948 she would rise to greatness again. Next day Goebbels sent me the horoscopes. I could not fathom everything in them; but in the subjoined interpretation, newly drawn up, I found it all; and now I am eagerly awaiting the second half of April."

H. R. Trevor-Roper, 1947 [27b]

Berliners take water from a bomb crater for cooking and household use.

### HITLER STAYS IN BERLIN

Eva Braun, Hitler's mistress, watches the Führer as he rests.

• Toward midnight Eva Braun sent an SS orderly to invite me to the small room

against everyone. Then he announced he planned to kill himself.

Depressed and downcast, yet infuriated by what he considered treachery, corruption, and failure on the part of the army, Hitler declared that he would remain in Berlin—rather than flee south—and would personally direct the defense of the city. The other people in the bunker, he said, could leave if they wanted; some, such as Himmler, Speer, Goering, and Ribbentrop, had left after the birthday party two days earlier. Others, including Eva Braun and the Goebbels family, would remain to the end.

in the bunker that was both her bedroom and living room. . . . "How about a bottle of champagne for our farewell? And some sweets? I'm sure you haven't eaten in a long time."

I was touched by her concern; she was the first person to think that I might be hungry after my many hours in the bunker. The orderly brought a bottle of Moet et Chandon, cake, and sweets. We remained alone. "You know, it was good that you came back once more. The Fuehrer had assumed you would be working against him. But your visit has proved the opposite to him, hasn't it?" I did not answer that question. "Anyhow, he liked what you said to him today. He has made up his mind to stay here, and I am staying with him. And you know the rest, too, of course. . . . He wanted to send me back to Munich. But I refused; I've come to end it here."

She was also the only person in the bunker capable of humane considerations. "Why do so many more people have to be killed?" she asked. "And it's all for nothing."

*Albert Speer, 1969* [25m]

## EVA BRAUN

• In the first half of the month of April [1945], Eva Braun unexpectedly and unbidden arrived in Berlin and declared that she would not leave Hitler's side again. Hitler urged her to return to Munich, and I too offered her a seat in our courier plane. But she obstinately refused, and everyone in the bunker knew why she had come. Figuratively and in reality, with her presence a messenger of death moved into the bunker.

*Albert Speer, 1969* [25n]

• For more than twelve years she had been his mistress. . . .

She is interesting for her role in the last chapter of this narrative but not interesting in herself; she was not a Pompadour or a Lola Montez. Hitler, although he was undoubtedly extremely fond of her and found relaxation in her unobstrusive company, had always kept her out of sight,

The last known picture of Hitler: Accompanied by the leader of the Hitler Youth, he awards decorations to German youngsters.

refusing to allow her to come to his various headquarters, where he spent almost all of his time during the war years, and rarely permitting her even to come to Berlin. She remained immured at the Berghof on the Obersalzberg, passing her time in swimming and skiing, in reading cheap novels and seeing trashy films, in dancing (which Hitler disapproved of) and endlessly grooming herself, pining away for her absent loved one.

*William L. Shirer, 1960* [24t]

## ALLIED FORCES ATTACK BERLIN

● Of Hitler at least it can be said that his emotions were genuine. He at least intended to die if Berlin fell. And yet,—such was the extraordinary confidence which still alternated with his despair,—even now he still believed that the city might be saved. Though he was prepared to die if it fell, nevertheless it seemed impossible that the capital of the Reich really could fall with the Fuehrer inside it. He regarded himself, it seems, as a kind of palladium, a totem whose presence rendered any citadel impregnable, so long as he stayed. "If I leave East Prussia," he told Keitel at Rastenburg, "then East Prussia will fall; if I stay, it will be held." Keitel had persuaded him to leave East Prussia, and East Prussia had duly fallen; but he did not intend to leave Berlin, and Berlin therefore could not fall.

*H. R. Trevor-Roper, 1947* [27d]

● In the final weeks Hitler lost not only his powers of resistance but also much of his former decisiveness and intellectual energy. This may have been because he, like others, was not equal to the terrible strain, but it may also have resulted from the continual use of drugs. At any rate it was obvious that it was not only his body which was showing symptoms of breakdown, but his mind too. The shaking of his head and the trembling of the left side of his body, which was especially apparent in his arm and hand, were increasing. His movements have become still more shambling, his posture more bent.

At dawn on April 24, Hitler received a telegram from Goering: "In view of your decision to remain at your post in the fortress of Berlin, do you agree that I take over, at once, the total leadership of the Reich, with full freedom of action at home and abroad, as your deputy, in accordance with your decree of 29 June 1941? If no reply is received by ten o'clock tonight, I shall take it for granted that you have lost your freedom of action, and shall consider the conditions of your decree as fulfilled, and shall act for the best interests of our country and our people." [27e]

Hitler flew into a rage, stripped Goering of all authority and

When walking, he would place his right hand on his left, and when sitting, he would cross his right leg over his left, in order to conceal the trembling of his limbs from others. . . .

. . . "How long do you think the battle here will last?" I asked Bernd [on April 23, 1945].

He replied, "Eight, at the most ten days."

"You think there's absolutely no hope then?"

"None at all, only the possibility of dragging out this struggle for Berlin for a few more days. There might still be just a glimmer of hope perhaps, if it wasn't for Hitler," he added bitterly. "Hitler still wants to attack, you know; he still hasn't entirely abandoned his plan to attack and regain the Oder line later on!"

*Gerhard Boldt, 1947* [2d]

Bormann, succeeded in representing the matter as a kind of *coup d'état*. With a few whispered words, he incited Hitler to one of his grand outbursts. Hitler denounced Göring for laziness and failure, accused him of having "made corruption in our state possible" by his example, called him a drug addict, and finally—in a radio message written by Bormann— stripped him of all his offices and privileges. Then, exhausted and with an expression of dull satisfaction, he slumped back into his apathetic state and added contemptuously: "Well, all right, Let Göring negotiate the surrender. If the war is lost anyhow, it doesn't matter who does it."

*Joachim C. Fest, 1973* [6m]

## GOERING'S TELEGRAM

• . . . Göring's old antagonist, Martin

• [Hitler asked General Ritter von Greim] if he knew why he had been summoned. Greim did not know. "Because Hermann Goering has betrayed both me and his Fatherland," Hitler explained.

charged him with high treason. The following day Hitler distributed vials of cyanide to the people who remained in the bunker. On the evening of April 28, news of more "treachery" arrived. It was learned that Himmler had contacted Swedish diplomat Count Bernadotte and was attempting to negotiate a surrender in the West to U.S. General Dwight D. Eisenhower. Hitler was enraged, shocked, and soon sought revenge. "A traitor must never be my successor as Führer," he said. Hermann Fegelein, a Himmler aide still in the bunker, was shot to death. Himmler, in absentia, was given the same sentence.

Early on the morning of April 29, Hitler married Eva Braun

---

"Behind my back he has established connexions with the enemy. His action was a mark of cowardice! And against my orders he has sent me a disrespectful telegram, saying that I once named him as my successor, and that now, since I can no longer rule from Berlin, he is ready to rule from Berchtesgaden in my place. He closes the telegram by saying that if he had no answer from me by 9.30 that night,[7] he would take my assent for granted!"

As Hitler spoke, there were tears in his eyes. His head sagged; his face was white; and when he handed Goering's fatal telegram to Greim to read, it fluttered with the trembling of his hands. While Greim read, Hitler watched, breathing hard in short, convulsive puffs. The muscles in his face twitched. Suddenly he screamed:

"An ultimatum! a crass ultimatum! Nothing now remains! nothing is spared me! no loyalty is kept, no honour observed; there is no bitterness, no betrayal that has not been heaped upon me; and now this! It is the end. No injury has been left undone!"

*H. R. Trevor-Roper, 1947* [27f]

## HIMMLER'S DEFECTION

● . . . Lorenz had brought from the Propaganda Ministry the British Reuter report of Himmler's negotiations with Count Bernadotte. In the Bunker, Lorenz found Bormann, Goebbels, and Hewel sitting together, and to them he gave one copy of the text. They told him that Hitler was in conference with Ritter von Greim. He therefore gave a second copy to Heinz Linge, Hitler's personal servant, to be handed to the Fuehrer.

The scene which followed the delivery of that note has been variously described, according to the opportunities of knowledge, and the resources of vocabulary, possessed by the various witnesses of it. All agree that it was a dramatic scene. Hitler was white with indignation. This was the last, the unkindest cut of all: *der treue Heinrich*—faithful Heinrich—had betrayed him; the one Nazi leader whose loyalty had always been above suspicion had now stabbed him in the back. As the news spread round the Bunker, the obedient chorus again echoed the voice of its

in a ceremony eerily punctuated by the boom of artillery fire. Bormann and Goebbels acted as witnesses. A few bottles of champagne were uncorked and, while the guests talked about better days, the Führer retired to his room and dictated his personal and political testament to a secretary. In this document Hitler defended his career: "In these three decades I have been actuated solely by love and loyalty to my people. . . . It is untrue that I, or anyone else in Germany, wanted the war in 1939. It was desired and instigated solely by those international statesmen who were either of Jewish descent or worked for Jewish interests. I have made too many offers for the con-

leader, and men and women competed to denounce the traitor. Then Hitler withdrew with Bormann and Goebbels behind locked doors and a conference began.

. . . There can be no doubt that to Hitler the treachery of Himmler, as he conceived it to be, was the signal for the end.

*H. R. Trevor-Roper, 1947* [27g]

● This news upset Hitler far more than the alleged defection or even treachery of Hermann Göring. Göring's radio message had, at least, acknowledged Hitler's authority. Himmler, on the other hand, had totally ignored his Führer and acted completely independently over the most important issue of all. Moreover, Hitler had always thought of Himmler as his most loyal and devoted supporter and political ally. The last mainstay of whatever faith he may have had left in the loyalty and goodwill of his supporters now collapsed. He succumbed to a helpless paroxysm of rage, full of hate and contempt, such as few human beings can have experienced. He described Himmler's deceitful negotia-

tions as the most shameful betrayal in human history.

*Gerhard Boldt, 1947* [2e]

## THE MARRIAGE CEREMONY

● The formalities were brief. The two parties declared that they were of pure Aryan descent and were free from hereditary disease. In consequence of the military situation and other extraordinary circumstances, they proposed a war-time wedding, by simple word of mouth, and without any delay. In a few minutes the parties had given assent, the register had been signed, and the ceremony was over. . . .

. . . Thus, after many years, Eva Braun's position was at last defined. The ambiguity of her status was at last terminated; and when a servant, in a moment of crisis next day, broke the ban on speech with "E.B.," and addressed her as "Gnaediges Fraeulein," she could at last answer, "You may safely call me Frau Hitler." [15]

*H. R. Trevor-Roper, 1947* [27l]

trol and limitation of armaments, which posterity will not for all time be able to disregard, for the responsibility for the outbreak of this war to be laid on me." [4n]

In the will, Hitler named Admiral Karl Donitz as his successor. Goebbels was to be Chancellor and Bormann party minister. Seyss-Inquart, the Nazi Governor of Austria, would be Foreign Minister. Hitler asked them, and the German people, "to uphold the racial laws to the limit and to resist mercilessly the poisoner of all nations, international Jewry."

He also explained why he chose to commit suicide: "My wife and I chose to die in order to escape the shame of overthrow

● . . . the gruesome idea of having this wedding on the verge of a double suicide, as if he feared nothing so much as "illegitimacy" on his deathbed, marked the beginning of a trivial departure. It demonstrated how spent he was, drained of even his histrionic effects, even though the Wagnerian reminiscence of joining his beloved in death might in his eyes give the procedure a saving note of tragedy.

*Joachim C. Fest, 1973* [6n]

### HITLER'S DEATH

● Together with his wife, [Hitler] shook hands with all of them and then, mute and stooped, he vanished inside his room. And as though this life, which had so largely been governered by staged happenings and had always aimed at glaringly dramatic effects, could only end with a preposterous climax, at this time a dance began in the chancellery canteen (if we are to believe the accounts of the participants), a dance in which the weeks of

strained nerves sought violent release. Even repeated remonstrances that the Führer was about to die could not bring it to a halt.

*Joachim C. Fest, 1973* [6o]

● A tailor who had been employed in the Fuehrer's headquarters, and who was now immured with the rest in the Chancellery, was surprised when Brigadefuehrer Rattenhuber, the head of the police guard and a general in the S.S., slapped him cordially on the back and greeted him with democratic familiarity. In the strict hierarchy of the Bunker the tailor felt bewildered. It was as if he had been a high officer. "It was the first time I had ever heard a high officer say 'good evening,'" he said; "so I noticed that the mood had completely changed." Then, from one of his equals, he learned the reason of this sudden and irregular affiability. Hitler had said goodbye, and was going to commit suicide. There are few forces so solvent of class distinctions as common danger, and common relief. . . .

or capitulation. It is our wish that our bodies be burnt immediately in the place where I have performed the greater part of my daily work during the course of my twelve years' service to my people." [27h]

That day, news of Mussolini's death reached the bunker. And Hitler began to prepare for his own death. He tested the cyanide on his dog, Blondi. The chemical worked.

On April 30, with the Russians two city blocks from the bunker, Hitler and his wife retired to their room to find death. At 3:30 p.m., SS officers wrapped the two bodies in blankets and carried them out of the bunker. The corpses were deposited in a bomb

. . . A single shot was heard. After an interval they entered the suite. Hitler was lying on the sofa, which was soaked with blood. He had shot himself through the mouth. Eva Braun was also on the sofa, also dead. A revolver was by her side, but she had not used it; she had swallowed poison.

H R. Trevor-Roper, 1947 [27j]

## BURIED AMID THE RUBBLE

• Linge afterwards told one of the secretaries that they had been burned as Hitler had ordered, "till nothing remained"; but it is doubtful whether such total combustion could have taken place. 180 litres of petrol, burning slowly on a sandy bed, would char the flesh and dissipate the moisture of the bodies, leaving only an unrecognisable and fragile remainder; but the bones would withstand the heat.

H. R. Trevor-Roper, 1947 [27k]

• Long ago, in the days of struggle, Hitler had let himself be represented grandiloquently as "the man who would rather be a dead Achilles than a living dog." Later on, he had begun to elaborate the scenario for his obsequies. His burial place was to be a mighty crypt in the bell tower of the gigantic structure he had planned to build on the bank of the Danube at Linz. But in fact he was hastily shoveled into a shell hole among mountains of rubble, fragments of wall, cement mixers, and scattered rubbish.

Joachim C. Fest, 1973 [6p]

## NOW A PART OF HISTORY

• The first evidence of the changed atmosphere in the Bunker was noticed by the secretaries, who had been dismissed

crater, drenched with gasoline, and burned. Goebbels gave poison to his six children, then he and his wife killed themselves. Martin Bormann escaped—his fate is still unknown, though there is strong evidence that he died in Berlin during the closing days of the war. The other Nazi leaders met varying fates. Goering and Himmler committed suicide. Von Ribbentrop, Seyss-Inquart, and others were executed. Speer, Hess, and others served lengthy prison terms.

The battered garrison of Berlin surrendered on May 2, 1945. Five days later, Hitler's Germany—which was to have lasted 1,000 years—signed an unconditional surrender.

---

during the ceremony, but who now returned to their stations. On arrival they learned the details from Guensche and Linge; but it was not from such second-hand information only that they knew that Hitler was dead. Everyone, they observed, was smoking in the Bunker. During Hitler's lifetime that had been absolutely forbidden; but now the headmaster had gone and the boys could break the rules. Under the soothing influence of nicotine, whose absence must have increased the nervous tension of the past week, they were able to consider the administrative problems which the Fuehrer had left them to face.

*H. R. Trevor-Roper, 1947* [27e]

• History records no phenomenon like [Hitler]. Ought we to call him "great"? No one evoked so much rejoicing, hysteria, and expectation of salvation as he; no one so much hate. No one else produced, in a solitary course lasting only a few years, such incredible accelerations in the pace of history. No one else so changed the state of the world and left behind such a wake of ruins as he did. It took a coalition of almost all the world powers to wipe him from the face of the earth in a war lasting nearly six years, to kill him—to quote an army officer of the German resistance—"like a mad dog."

*Joachim C. Fest, 1973* [6j]

# CHRONOLOGY

**1889**

Apr. 20   Adolf Hilter born

**1903**

Jan. 3   Father, Alois, dies

**1907**

Oct.   Hitler moves to Vienna

Dec. 21   Mother, Klara, dies

**1913**

May   Hitler moves to Munich

**1914**

Aug. 1   World War I begins

Oct. 12   Hitler goes to front with the 1st Company, 16th Bavarian Reserve Infantry

**1916**

Oct. 7   Wounded in leg at Bapaume

**1917**

Mar.   Returns to front

Mar. 15   Czarist government collapes in Russia

**1918**

Mar. 3   Soviets sign Treaty of Brest-Litovsk

Mar. 7   German Workers' Party founded

Mar. 21   Germans launch last major offensive in the west

July   Foch launches Allied counteroffensive

Aug. 4   Hitler receives Iron Cross, First Class

Oct. 14   Temporarily blinded by gas attack

Oct. 30   Sailor's revolt at Kiel

Nov. 8   Council of Workers, Soldiers and Peasants declares Bavarian Republic at Munich

Nov. 9   Kaiser Wilhelm abdicates. Philipp Scheidemann declares the establishment of a Republic

Nov. 11   Germany signs Armistice

Dec.   Upon release from hospital, Hitler is stationed at Traunstein

**1919**

Jan.   Sparticist uprisings throughout Germany

Mar. 17   Government lifts martial law

Oct. 12   Hitler attends his first meeting of German Workers' Party

**1920**

Feb. 24   Organizes first rally of NSDAP

Apr. 1   Hitler resigns from the army

Dec.   NSDAP buys *Völkischer Beobachter*

### 1921

July 29  NSDAP invests full powers in Hitler, as chairman

Aug.  Hitler establishes party's "Gymnastic and Sports Division," forerunner of the SA

### 1922

Oct. 30  Mussolini's March on Rome

### 1923

Jan. 11  French troops enter the Rhineland because of Germany's failure to meet war debts

May 1  Hitler's attempt to break up May Day demonstration in Munich fails

Sept. 26  Reparation payments resume

Nov. 8-9  Hitler's Beerhall Putsch fails

Nov. 11  Imprisoned

### 1924

Feb. 26  Trial begins

Dec. 20  Hitler released from prison

### 1925

Feb. 27  Refounding of NSDAP

Apr. 7  Hitler gives up Austrian citizenship

Summer  Vol. I of *Mein Kampf* published

### 1926

Feb. 14  NSDAP meeting at Bamburg. Goebbels swears allegiance to Hitler; reconciliation of Hitler and Strasser

### 1929

Oct. 3  Chancellor, G. Stresseman, dies

### 1930

Mar. 13  Young Plan, reducing Germany's war indemnity, adopted

June 30  Otto Strasser and radical wing expelled from NSDAP

July 16  Reichstag dissolved for new elections

Sept. 14  Elections for seats in the Reichstag

### 1931

Oct. 10  Hitler's first meeting with Hindenburg

### 1932

Apr. 10  Run-off election between Hitler and Hindenburg for Presidency

May 30  Brüning resigns; Franz von Papen becomes Chancellor

June 4  Von Papen dissolves Reichstag

July  Ban on SA lifted

July 31  Elections; Nazis become largest party in the Reichstag

Aug. 13  Von Papen offers Hitler Vice-Chancellorship. Hitler demands Chancellorship; Hindenburg refuses

Sept. 12  Von Papen dissolves Reichstag

Nov.  Elections; Nazi vote decreases

Nov. 17  Von Papen resigns

Dec. 2  Kurt von Schleicher becomes Chancellor

### 1933

Jan. 4  Von Papen, Hitler, and German industrialists form political alliance at a secret meeting at a bank in Cologne

Jan. 21  Nationalists break their alliance with von Schleicher

Jan. 30  Hitler appointed Chancellor

Feb. 27  Reichstag Fire

Feb. 28  Decree "for the Protection of the People and the State" suspends many civil rights and becomes legal basis of Nazi regime

Mar. 5  Reichstag elections; NSDAP still short of majority

Mar. 23  Enabling Act, granting dictatorial powers to Hitler, passes Reichstag, 441-94

July 14  NSDAP declared only legal party

Oct. 14  Germany withdraws from League of Nations

### 1934

Jan. 26  Germany signs non-aggression pact with Poland

June 30  Party purge of SA (Night of the Long Knives)

July 25  Chancellor Dollfuss of Austria assassinated by Nazis, but putsch fails

**Aug. 2  Hindenburg dies; offices of Chancellor and President combined**

## 1935

Jan.  Plebiscite returns Saar to Germany

Sept.  Nuremberg Party Rally

Sept. 15  Promulgation of Nuremberg Laws against Jews

## 1936

Mar. 5  German troops reoccupy demilitarized Rhineland

July 17  Spanish Civil War begins

## 1937

Jan. 30  Hitler withdraws German signature from the Treaty of Versailles

## 1938

Feb. 11  Chancellor Kurt von Schuschnigg of Austria meets Hitler at Obersalzberg; Hitler demands annexation of Austria by Germany

Mar. 8  Schuschnigg announces plebiscite on the question of whether Austria wants to unite with German Reich

Mar. 11  German troops enter Austria

Mar. 14  Hitler arrives in Vienna

Sept. 15  Chamberlain hears Hitler's demands on Czechoslovakia at meeting at Berchtesgaden

Sept. 22  Chamberlain and Hitler meet at Godesberg

Sept. 29  Hitler, Mussolini, Daladier, and Chamberlain confer at Munich

Oct. 1  Germans occupy Sudetenland

Nov. 9  Crystal Night

## 1939

Mar. 15  Hitler enters Prague

May 21  Formal signing of "Pact of Steel" between Italy and Germany

Aug. 23  German-Soviet Pact signed

Sept. 1  German invasion of Poland

Sept. 3  Britain and France declare war on Germany

## 1940

Apr. 9  Germany invades Denmark and Norway

May 10  Germans invade low countries and move into France

May 23  French sign armistice, establishing occupied and unoccupied zones

Aug. 13  Bombing of English cities begins

## 1941

May 10  Rudolf Hess flies to Britain

June 22  Hitler attacks Soviet Union

Dec. 6  Soviets launch major counter-offensive; relieve pressure on Moscow

Dec. 7  Japan attacks Pearl Harbor; U.S. enters war

## 1942

Nov. 4  Rommel defeated at El Alamein

Nov. 8  Allies land in North Africa

## 1943

Jan. 31  Soviets capture and annihilate German Army at Stalingrad

July 10  Allies invade Sicily

July 25  Mussolini toppled and arrested

Sept. 12  SS detachment springs Mussolini from prison high in Abruzzi mountains

Sept. 15  Mussolini installed as dictator of German-occupied Northern Italy

## 1944

June 6  Allied invasion of Normandy

July 20  Attempt on Hitler's life by German officers fails

Aug. 24  Goebbels orders call-up of all men between the ages of 15 and 60

Aug. 25  Liberation of Paris

Dec. 16  Battle of the Bulge begins

## 1945

April 13  U.S. President, Franklin D. Roosevelt, dies

Apr. 28  Partisans capture and, 2 days later, kill Benito Mussolini, who tried to escape to Switzerland

Apri. 29  Hitler marries Eva Braun

Apri. 30  At 3:30 p.m., Berlin time . . . Hitler and his wife commit suicide

# BIBLIOGRAPHY

The source of a quotation, if not completely identified at the end of the quotation, is indicated by a superscript that follows the author's name and the date of the quotation. For example, on page 2, the source of the first quote is Joachim C. Fest, 1973 [6a]. The "6" in [6a] refers to the sixth book listed below; the "a" gives the page number in the Fest book where the quotation can be found.

1. Baynes, Norman H., ed. *The Speeches of Adolf Hitler, April 1922-August 1939.* Howard Fertig, N.Y., 1969. (Originally published by Oxford Univ. Press under the auspices of The Royal Institute of International Affairs)
   a-117; b-855; c-289.
2. Boldt, Gerhard. *Hitler: The Last Ten Days.* Coward, McCann & Geoghegan, N.Y., 1973. (First publication, *Die letzten Tage der Reichskanzlei,* Rowohlt Verlag GmbH, Germany, 1947) Copyright © 1973 by Arthur Barker Ltd.
   a-44; b-62; c-92, 93; d-82, 160; e-193-194.
3. Bracher, Karl Dietrich. *The German Dictatorship: The Origins, Structure, and Effects of National Socialism.* (Trans. by Jean Steinberg) Praeger, N.Y., 1970. (First publication, *Die deutsche Diktatur: Entstehung, Struktur, Folgen des Nationalsozialismus,* Verlag Kiepenheuer & Witsch, Germany, 1969)
   a-157, 158; b-254; c-418-419.
4. Bullock, Alan. *Hitler: A Study in Tyranny.* Harper & Row, N.Y., 1964. (© 1962, A. Bullock)
   a-80; b-120; c-121; d-121; e-71; f-200; g-256-257; h-278-279; i-356; j-357; k-379; l-90-91; m-470; n-793-794; o-628, 629; p-691; q-688; r-689-690; s-690-691.
5. Calic, Edouard, ed. *Secret Conversations with Hitler: The Two Newly-Discovered 1931 Interviews.* John Day, N.Y., 1971. (Copyright © 1971 by Chatto & Windus Ltd.) From Richard Breiting's shorthand notes taken during interviews with Hitler. Breiting, a German journalist, was eventually found suspect by the Nazis and, in 1937, was poisoned by Gestapo agents. The notes of the two interviews had been hidden with his sister.
   a-17; b-22, 32, 39-40.

6. Fest, Joachim C. *Hitler*. (Trans. by Richard and Clara Winston) Harcourt Brace Jovanovich, N.Y., 1974. (Copyright © 1973 by Verlag Ullstein; Copyright © 1974 by Harcourt Brace Jovanovich)
   a-6; b-24-25; c-32, 57; d-56; e-146; f-187, 188; g-269, 270; h-287, 288; i-382; j-3; k-639; l-638; m-740; n-745; o-748; p-749.

7. François-Poncet, André. *The Fateful Years: Memoirs of a French Ambassador in Berlin, 1931-1938*. (Trans. by Jacques LeClercq) Howard Fertig, N.Y., 1972. (First publication, *Souvenirs d'une Ambassade à Berlin*, France, 1946)
   a-52, 54, 55; b-78; c-179; d-237.

8. Heiden, Konrad. *Der Fuehrer: Hitler's Rise to Power*. (Trans. by Ralph Manheim) Beacon Press, Boston, 1969. (© 1944, K. Heiden)
   b-131; c-204, 205; d-205; e-206-207.

9. Heiden, Konrad. *A History of National Socialism*. (Trans. by Ian F. B. Morrow) Alfred A. Knopf, N.Y., © 1935, 1963. (First publications, *Geschichte des Nationalsozialismus*, 1932, and *Geburt des dritten Reiches*, 1934)
   a-51-52; b-79.

10. Heiden, Konrad. *Hitler: A Biography*. (Trans. by Winifred Ray) Alfred A. Knopf, N.Y., © 1936, 1964. (First publication, *Adolf Hitler: Das Zeitalter der Verantwortungslosigkeit. Eine Biographie*, Europa-Verlag, 1936)
    a-8; b-21; c-50, 52; d-45; e-53; f-96-97; g-221; h-87; i-79, 86.

11. Hitler, Adolf. *Mein Kampf*. (Trans. by Ralph Manheim) Houghton Mifflin, Boston, 1943. (First ©, 1925, by Verlag Frz. Eher Nachf, GmbH, Germany)
    a-4; b-14-15; c-8, 17, 18; d-56, 57; e-204, 205, 206; f-218-219; g-222, 223; h-179-180, 184; i-3.

12. *Hitler's Secret Conversations*. (Trans. by Norman Cameron and R. H. Stevens) Farrar, Straus and Young, N.Y., 1953.
    a-292; b-293; c-198; d-335; e-527; f-232; g-342-343; h-332, 333; i-6; j-355; k-11; l-382; m-356; n-341; o-9; p-354; q-224; r-12; s-13; t-343; u-165; v-506; w-564; x-341-342; y-289; z-167; aa-72; bb-96, 97.

13. Heiber, Helmut. *Adolf Hitler*. (Trans. by Lawrence Wilson) Oswald Wolff (Publishers) Ltd., London, 1961. (First published in German by Colloquium Verlag Otto H. Hess, Berlin-Dahlem, © 1960)
    a-10; b-14-15; c-30; d-36; e-68-69; f-73.

14. Hoffmann, Heinrich. *Hitler Was My Friend*. Burke, London, 1955.
    a-71-72; b-71; c-115; d-160-161.

15. Jetzinger, Franz. *Hitler's Youth*. Hutchinson, London, 1958.
    a-56-57; b-59; c-135.

16. Kubizek, August. *Young Hitler: The Story of our Friendship*. Allan Wingate, London, 1954.
    a-30; b-135; c-31; d-87, 91.

17. Maser, Werner. *Hitler: Legend, Myth & Reality*. (Trans. by Peter and Betty Ross) Harper & Row, N.Y., 1973. (First publication, *Adolf Hitler: Legende, Mythos, Wirklichkeit*, Bechtle Verlag, Germany, 1971)
    a-157; b-43; c-71; d-88; e-191; f-121; g-203; h-202; i-207.

18. Goebbels, Joseph. *The Goebbels Diaries: 1942-1943*. (Ed. + trans. by Louis P. Lochner) Doubleday, Garden City, 1948. (Translation © 1948 by The Fireside Press, Inc.)
    a-64; b-49; c-225; d-35; e-396-397; f-483; g-311; h-404.

19. Miller, Douglas. *You Can't Do Business with Hitler*. Little, Brown, Boston, 1941.
    a-96; b-6, 16.

20. Mowrer, Edgar Ansel. *Germany Puts The Clock Back* (revised edition). William Morrow, N.Y., 1939. (First publication, 1933)
    a-235, 236-237.
21. *Nazi Conspiracy and Aggression,* Volume 6. U.S. Government Printing Office, Washington, 1946. This 10-volume publication contains documents, affidavits, and interrogations collected for the Nuremberg trial.
    a-635; b-787ff.
22. Prange, Gordon W., ed. *Hitler's Words.* American Council on Public Affairs, Washington, D.C., 1944.
    a-225; b-246; c-230; d-203; e-216; f-122; g-83; h-38; i-39; j-4; k-10, 11; l-42; m-5; n-81-82; o-42, 43; p-43; q-18-19; r-23; s-27; t-162; u-163; v-112-113; w-283; x-236; y-114; z-261; aa-270; bb-270; cc-171; dd-216.
23. Rauschning, Hermann. *The Revolution of Nihilism: Warning to the West.* (Trans. by E. W. Dickes) Alliance Book, N.Y., 1939.
    a-15, 19, 23; b-16; c-49; d-78; e-48; f-237.
24. Shirer, William L. *The Rise and Fall of the Third Reich.* Simon and Schuster, N.Y., 1960. (© 1959, 1960 by William L. Shirer)
    a-25; b-46; c-46-47; d-62; e-74; f-75; g-82; h-81; i-192, 194; j-223; k-389; l-397; m-415-416; n-742-743; o-776, 777; p-762; q-837; r-871; s-1069; t-1111; u-347.
25. Speer, Albert. *Inside the Third Reich.* (Trans. by R. and C. Winston) The Macmillan Co., N.Y., 1970. (First publication, *Erinnerungen,* Verlag Ullstein GmbH, Germany, 1969)
    a-72; b-73; c-161-162; d-220; e-174-175, 176; f-440; g-254, 306; h-305, 306; i-370-371; j-357; k-389; l-355; m-484; n-465.
26. Strasser, Otto. *Hitler and I.* (Trans. by Gwenda David and Eric Mosbacher) Houghton Mifflin, Boston, 1940.
    a-62-63.
27. Trevor-Roper, H. R. *The Last Days of Hitler.* Collier Books, N.Y., 1966. (© 1947, 1962 by H. R Trevor-Roper)
    a-114; b-160; c-265-266; d-222; e-192-193; f-211-212; g-229; h-240-241; i-234, 235; j-257-258, 260; k-264.
28. *Trial of Major War Criminals Before the International Military Tribunal.* 42 vols., Nuremberg, 1947-1949.
    a-vol. 31, p. 446ff; b-vol. 7, p. 584.
29. Wheeler-Bennett, John W. *The Nemesis of Power.* The Viking Press, N.Y., 1967. (© 1964 by Sir John Wheeler-Bennett)
    a-15; b-339, 340, 373; c-144-145.
30. Fischer, Louis. *Men and Politics.* Duell, Sloan and Pearce, N.Y., 1941.
    a-23; b-23-24; c-114-115; d-167.
31. Gordon, Harold J., Jr. *Hitler and the Beer Hall Putsch.* Princeton Univ., Princeton, Copyright © 1972.
    a-389; b-49; c-364-365; d-364; e-618-619; f-482; g-618.
32. Smith, Bradley F. *Adolf Hitler; His Family, Childhood and Youth.* The Hoover Institution on War, Revolution and Peace, Stanford, 1967.
    a-37, 50; b-41-42; c-58-59; d-79; e-92; f-92; g-137; h-117-118; i-153.
33. Waldman, Morris D. *Sieg Heil! The Story of Adolf Hitler.* Oceana Publications, Dobbs Ferry, 1962. (Copyright © 1962 by Morris D. Waldman)
    a-23; b-30; c-31; d-96; e-97.

# INDEX